KT-406-280

Selim Aga
A Slave's Odyssey

By the same author:

Scotland: The Land and Its Uses, Chambers Harrap, 1994
Scotland, Land and People, Luath Press, 1998
Wild Scotland, Luath Press, 1998, revised 2006
Journey into Africa: The Life and Death of Keith Johnston, Scottish Cartographer and Explorer (1844–79) Whittles Publishing, 2004
The Road to Tanganyika: The Diaries of Donald Munro and William McEwan, Kachere Series, 2006

Selim Aga
A Slave's Odyssey

JAMES McCARTHY

Luath Press Limited
EDINBURGH
www.luath.co.uk

First published 2006

ISBN (10): 1-905222-17-3
ISBN (13): 978-1-905222-17-9

The paper used in this book is recyclable.
It is made from low-chlorine pulps produced in a low-energy, low-emission manner from renewable forests.

The publisher acknowledges subsidy from

towards the publication of this volume.

Printed and bound by Creative Print and Design, Ebbw Vale

Typeset in 11 point Sabon

For Brody and Kit

Acknowledgements

IN THE RESEARCH for this work I am pleased to acknowledge the financial support of the Carnegie Trust for the Universities of Scotland which enabled me to visit a number of relevant institutions in London and to the Strathmartine Trust for a grant to cover the costs of illustrations. I am particularly indebted to the National Library of Scotland and I have been considerably assisted by the librarians of both Aberdeen City Council and Aberdeenshire Information Services.

Andrew Thurburn generously provided background material on his great-great-grandfather Robert Thurburn of Alexandria. Marion Walls of Kirkintilloch kindly supplied details of her family's direct genealogical links to Selim, as did Don Crevie of Seattle. Yassir Abidi Berdewil has stimulated interest in the Sudanese connection by publishing parts of the story in Arabic on a Sudanese website. Jennie Renton and my son-in-law Jonathan Falla have taken considerable time and care in editing the manuscript, and I am also grateful to Jonathan for bringing to my attention *Poems on the Abolition of the Slave Trade* by James Montgomery, James Grahame, and E Benger (1809). I have abstracted freely from this extraordinary work to provide the verses quoted at the head of each chapter. I relied upon Tony Reid's genealogical expertise to obtain essential records. My special thanks go to my wife for her encouragement and not a little forbearance throughout the extended gestation period of this work.

I am especially grateful to Mrs Jinx Rodger for permission to use illustrations from *Village of the Nubas* by George Rodger and to John Hare for permission to use illustrations from *Shadows Across the Sahara* (2001). Thanks also to the McManus Galleries, Dundee City Council Leisure and Arts, and to George D Lintzeris of Petra Fine Arts and Andrew Thurburn for the photographs of himself with a portrait of Robert Thurburn and of Selim Aga's inscription. Andrew Gorzalka kindly digitised a number of the illustrations.

Contents

Illustrations
Black and White

Plates

Author's Note to Selected Illustrations

PLATES 4 AND 5: The superb photographs of the Nuba, taken in 1949 by George Rodger, are unique. Rodger was born in Selkirk. After a distinguished career as a war photographer, he founded the famous Magnum photographic agency with Henri Cartier Bresson, David Seymour and Robert Capa and his work was used regularly by *Life* magazine. In an extended journey through Africa in the late 1940s, Rodger was fascinated by the Nuba of the Sudan, with whom he spent six weeks. He was the first to document the tribes of that region when they were largely untouched by Western civilisation, and not dissimilar in their lifestyle and customs from Selim's time. His photographic essay, *Le Village des Noubas,* first appeared in 1955 and was republished by Phaidon in 1999. George Rodger died in 1995 aged eighty-seven.

The former Nazi filmmaker Leni Riefenstahl visited the area in the mid-1950s and her striking photographic images of the Nuba people were widely circulated. The erosion of the Nuba way of life subsequently caused by tourism has been exacerbated by the policies of the Islamic government of Sudan towards these tribes.

PLATES 6, 7 AND 8: The Scottish artist David Roberts painted his acclaimed pictures of Egypt and the Holy Land in 1838 close to the period when Selim was in Cairo and Alexandria. Roberts was appalled by his encounters with slaves but his illustrations of the slave market and Cairo seem somewhat sanitised. He was able to depict the antiquities of the Nile, such as the fabulous painted columns of the temple at Karnak, close to their original colours which they then still retained and which Selim saw on his trip with the Thurburns.

The painting of the interview with Muhammed Ali at his palace in Alexandria includes the British Consul Patrick Campbell, Lieutenant Wagstaffe of the Overland Transit Company, David Roberts himself (he painted the scene from memory), and two English officers. Robert Thurburn would have been present at many such interviews. Interestingly, Roberts also made contributions to the 'Panorama of the Nile', with which Selim was associated as lecturer. The original David Roberts lithographs were photographed and are reproduced here by kind permission of George D Lintzeris of Petra Fine Arts, Baltimore, Maryland.

PLATE 10: Thomas Faed was noted for his scenes of humble rural life in Scotland; it was said that he had done for Scottish art what Robert Burns had done for Scottish song. His famous picture, *The Visit of the Patron and Patroness to the Village School,* was exhibited in London in 1852, not long after Selim attended a similar school in Aberdeenshire. In many ways it represents his experience, except in one particular: it is obvious that here, the former slave boy – in slightly superior attitude in his fine blue coat – is not an attendee (emphasised by the jealous aggression of the child behind him), and is probably a servant or valet. The patron and patroness could well have been the Thurburns from Murtle House. Although the schoolroom Faed depicts is relatively well furnished by the standards of the time, the age range and poverty of some of the children is typical of a rural school of the mid-nineteenth century.

Further Sources of Illustrations

Life of Captain Sir Richard Burton (1898) Lady Isabel Burton (see pp 144, 185, plate 14)
Abeokuta and the Camaroons Mountains: An Exploration (1863) Richard Burton (see pp 161, 186)
Sudan Notes & Records 19, 1948 (see p 20)
Poems on the Abolition of the Slave Trade (1809) James Montgomery (see pp 35, 106)
Shadows Across the Sahara (2001) John Hare (plate 3)
Life in Victorian London (1973) LCB Seaman (see p 121)
The Search for the Niger (1973) C Lloyd (see pp 131, 134, 139)
Dahomey and the Dahomans (1851) FE Forbes (plates 12 and 13)
Le Desert et le Soudan (1853) Comte Stanislas d'Escayrac de Lauture (see p 38)
Africa Considered in its Social and Political Condition, with a Plan for the Amelioration of its Inhabitants (1853) Selim Aga (see pp 122, 123)

Foreword

THIS BOOK FILLS another space in a complex jigsaw puzzle, the history of Scotland's centuries-old interaction with Africa and Africans. When I was researching the historical material for my novel *Joseph Knight* I felt very much as if I were hunting for an individual who, though a key figure in that history, had become hidden from us over time. Joseph Knight, at the Court of Session in 1778, successfully established not only that he should not be the slave of the planter John Wedderburn, but also that no individual, regardless of race, creed or colour, could be a slave in Scotland. Ironically, we know nothing of his life after he won his freedom. James McCarthy, in reconstructing the life of Selim Aga, has had an equally intriguing hunt, with its own rewards and frustrations, but the story he reveals is fascinating both for its historical background and as a record of one individual's courage, versatility, strength and, against all the odds, survival into his late forties.

Sixty years after the Knight v. Wedderburn case, Selim Aga, like Joseph was enslaved while still a young boy. But Selim's oppressors were Arab slavers and it was his purchase by a Scot, Robert Thurburn, the British Consul in Alexandria, that effectively liberated him. Selim's ensuing relationship with Scotland seems to have been one of mutual benefit and satisfaction. Certainly it was much to be welcomed by Selim after his ordeal as a kidnapped child – forced to travel 2,000 miles from his native Sudan to Egypt, subjected to terrible brutality *en route*, and changing hands no fewer than nine times before being rescued by Thurburn. That Selim survived at all is remarkable. That he went on to experience life on Thurburn's Aberdeenshire estate, and to have numerous other adventures before becoming steward to the explorer Sir Richard Burton, makes for a story that is truly astonishing.

Selim Aga was clearly a talented, humane, good-humoured man who doggedly overcame all the obstacles life placed in his way, and I am delighted to have made his acquaintance in the pages of James McCarthy's book.

James Robertson, Newtyle, Angus

INTRODUCTION
Searching for Selim

Britannia... She shared the gain, the glory, and the guilt,
By her were Slavery's island altars built,
And fed with human victims; – till the cries
Of blood, demanding vengeance from the skies,
Pierced her proud heart, too long in vain assail'd;
But justice in one glorious hour prevail'd:
Straight from her limbs the tyrant's garb she tore...
Then plunged them in th' abysses of the sea,
And cried to weeping Africa – 'Be free!'

I FIRST ENCOUNTERED Selim Aga by chance. Researching a different topic in the *Geographical Magazine* of 1875, I noticed in an adjacent column a letter from the renowned explorer Sir Richard Burton. In the way that one can become sidetracked in libraries, I read on. Burton was at pains to refute speculation that an article which had appeared in the journal in 1874 was not by its stated author, Selim Aga. *Queen* magazine had insisted that the work was 'manifestly the work of a cultivated European.'[1] Certainly 'My Parentage and Early Career as a Slave' is expressed in faultless idiomatic English.[2] It tells the extraordinary story of a boy, born and brought up in the Kingdom of Taqali in the Nuba Mountains of southern Sudan, being captured by Arab slavers; after a journey of over 2,000 miles through the Sudan and Egypt, and many adventures, he was sold as a slave in the Cairo market, to be purchased subsequently by the British Consul in Alexandria, Robert Thurburn, who brought him back to Scotland in 1836. There Selim's account, which is full of fascinating – and sometimes horrifying – detail, ends. With an interest in the Scottish connection with Africa, I was intrigued and determined to find out more.

In his letter to the *Geographical Magazine*, Burton provides a brief biography of Selim, whom he had recruited in Lagos as his manservant in 1861 and who accompanied him throughout his West African travels conducted during the three years when he was British Consul on the island of Fernando Po.[3] Burton knew both John Thurburn, a rich trader in Alexandria, and his younger brother, Robert; the latter had helped Burton make preparations for his famous secret journey to Mecca in disguise in 1853. Another of Burton's friends in Alexandria was John Wingfield Larking, John Thurburn's son-in-law, who was the first to take in hand Selim's education in English. There is a certain symmetry in the fact that Selim should be linked to two British consuls appointed to quite separate parts of the continent, but who were very different in temperament and personality.

Selim's Thurburn connections would have recommended him to Burton, who in any case favoured Africans of apparently Arab origin over so-called Negroes, and who attests that in the course of a number of arduous journeys in West Africa he proved to be everything a gentleman could have wished for in a manservant. Burton compares him to Figaro, but nowadays he might have described him as a 'Jeeves'. In an article for the Royal Geographical Society in 1862, Burton refers to:

> my steward, Selim Agha, an invaluable man, a native of Tegulet, and a protégé of the late venerable Mr Robert Thurburn, of Alexandria. He had spent a dozen years of his life at a school in Scotland, where he learned to cook, doctor, spin, carpenter, shoot, collect specimens, and stuff birds – briefly, everything.[4]

Starting with Burton's claim in his letter to the *Geographical Magazine* that Selim went to School at 'Murtho', I attempted to locate this in Scotland, and failed. But Burton provided a clue when he said that Selim spoke 'English', or rather, 'Scotch' with the true Lowland accent, which inspired me to experiment with pronouncing 'Murtho' in the back of the throat. In this way, I came up with something sounding like 'Murtle'. When a search of the gazetteers indicated that such a place existed just west of Aberdeen, and that in the 1830s it was owned by a John Thurburn, merchant of Alexandria, another piece of the jigsaw fell into place.

An internet search subsequently yielded another, similar version of Selim's early life, published in an electronic edition of 2003 by the Chapel Hill Library of the University of North Carolina. This website also displays the original title page of *Incidents Connected with the Life of Selim Aga, A Native of Central Africa,* dedicated to Mrs Thurburn of Murtle and privately printed in 1846 by W Bennett of Aberdeen. It transpires that a London edition of this 45-page booklet was issued by John K Chapman and Co in 1850.

According to the author's preface, Selim had been persuaded by friends to write this vivid fragment of biography. It is clear from the fulsome dedication to Mrs Thurburn, wife of John Thurburn, that he regarded her as a true mother substitute, and she in turn might well have treated him as the son she never had. It differs only slightly from the version which appeared almost thirty years later in the *Geographical Magazine* and I have drawn from both versions to describe Selim's early experiences. I have also used his own spelling of his name, ie without the 'h' which Burton frequently uses. In Arabic, the term ʿaga' or 'agha' is used to denote rank. The names 'Selim' and 'Agha' or 'Aga' were common throughout the Ottoman Empire in the nineteenth century, but are unlike any native names from Selim's home district; it is doubtful that this was his original name and it may well have been given to him by the slavers, who usually gave their charges Arabic names, as well as ensuring that they were circumcised.

Selim's narrative and the wealth of detail he supplies may seem incredible in the recollection of a boy, by his own account, aged around eight years old. However, he lived in a community which was entirely oral in its culture, where stories would be told and retold, and where, without written records, there was complete dependence on memory; even at his tender age, his own observation and memory would have been well developed, and his subsequent education shows him to be a very intelligent young man. Compared to his British equivalent he would have been mature for his years – he had, after all, been on a hunting expedition before he was eight years old, and at much the same age was introduced to his prospective bride. By his own assessment, he was a seasoned traveller and cameleer before he had reached his teens.

What do we know of Selim Aga's abilities and character? His own narrative suggests considerable resilience of mind and body, while Burton gives an impression of an individual endowed with great energy and courage, real leadership qualities and authority – and there is no doubt that working for this notoriously irascible taskmaster would have demanded patience, tact, and adaptability. Whether Selim was naturally serious or happy in outlook, whether he made friends easily or was difficult to reach – such aspects of his personality are not discernible with so little to go on. He undoubtedly had imagination and some romantic feelings, as expressed in his early poems, and perhaps also a certain impetuousness combined with a wanderlust which would take him to many parts of the world.

He was in fact following the precept of one of the earliest of world travellers, the Arab Ibn Batuta: 'He who does not travel knows not the value of man.' During his time in London he would have developed the art of public speaking and, consequently, his own confidence. He appears to have adopted European customs and mores completely, and that he identified himself with the patriotism and hubris of Victorian Britain is reflected in his early poetry; whether he changed his views in later life as a result of his experiences is not known. Nor do we know whether he was ambivalent about his own identity, as a black living in a European-dominated society, even in the Africa of the time.

The picture of Selim's life that emerges from the available sources is evocative, for all that it is very incomplete. There is a complete dearth of information between his arrival in Scotland around 1836 and his departure for London in 1849. Apart from a census entry, there is no mention in any local records of his stay at Murtle, which is particularly surprising since he would certainly have been something of a curiosity. It was only through the discovery in the British Library of a pamphlet written by Selim in 1853 that I came to know that he spent several years in London. There is a solitary reference to his time with the Niger expedition of 1857, and we are dependent on Burton's sparse mentions of him for the years 1861 to 1864; there follows another blank until his death, reportedly in Liberia in 1875. His 'worldwide travels' alluded to by Burton may have taken place in this final period, or in his youth with John Thurburn.

Apart from *Incidents* and the 1853 pamphlet outlining his plan to establish free trade in Africa – *Africa Considered in its Social and Political Condition, with a Plan for the Amelioration of its Inhabitants* – I have been unable to identify anything further published by Selim, other than possibly his description of a trip up the Congo. Burton had ended his description of Selim in the *Geographical Magazine* with the words:

> And now my factotum shall speak for himself. I leave his manuscript at the office of the *Geographical Magazine*, to prevent all suspicion of its being written by any one but 'Selim Agha'.[5]

There is a conundrum here. The posthumous publication *Wanderings in Three Continents,* attributed to Burton but edited by WH Wilkins, which appeared in 1901, contains a chapter entitled 'A Trip up the Congo', which Wilkins claims was written by him from notes roughly jotted down by Burton in a memorandum book. Wilkins states that he 'thought it best to publish them as they stood, with no alterations except those necessary to make the essay coherent and legible'. However, the chapter contains considerable chunks of Selim's account word for word, although there are differences. For example, Selim's record (Appendix 2) is impersonal and factual, and omits the characteristic vituperation and bitter comments about the behaviour of the Congolese attributed to Burton in the 1901 publication.

One interpretation might be that Selim has plagiarised Burton's work (or at least his notes) albeit with Burton's apparent connivance, but this gesture would have been uncharacteristic of Burton, who was not disposed to let anyone else steal his thunder. Moreover Burton, in 1876, published his own very full account of the trip, the two-volume *Two Trips to Gorilla Land and the Cataracts of the Congo,* in which he specifically refers to Selim's previously published record in the *Geographical Magazine*. Burton on two occasions therefore confirms that Selim is the author of the article in question, despite its close similarity to his own 'rough notes' – if indeed they were his. (In fact, the relevant chapter in *Wanderings,* despite the editor's assertion, appears more like a finished essay.) What is even more curious, is why the editor should have chosen to use these notes rather than to quarry the much fuller and quite comprehensive volume two of *Two Trips* published twenty-five years previously.

There are all sorts of possible explanations, but it is highly unlikely that Burton would have risked his reputation, about which he was inordinately jealous, to assert Selim's authorship. It begs the question of why he should contemplate this subterfuge, unless he gave Selim access to these notes as part recompense for most faithful service. It is the case that Burton was something of a joker and had previously attributed his own writing to another, no doubt out of a sense of mischief. This question, which to my knowledge has not been revealed before now, appears likely to remain an intriguing mystery. That puzzle, however, does not cast any doubt on the authenticity of Selim's *Incidents* or his authorship of the original *Geographical Magazine* article.

Selim's story has to be seen against the background of the international slave trade, an issue which created huge divisions in British society, with moral repugnance against the traffic in human souls matched by its fierce defence from those who saw its cessation as undermining swathes of the expanding national economy. The public debates were long and bitter. Burton himself, as a consul, was required by the British Government to assist in persuading chiefs to cease slave trading, supported by a squadron of Royal Navy ships which patrolled off the coast of both East and West Africa, and yet he was clearly ambivalent on the question. He was positively damning about the 'airs and graces' which he claimed liberated slaves, such as the Sierra Leonians, gave themselves and regarded anti-slavery societies as too liberal by half. Selim, on the other hand, not surprisingly, takes a different view in the preface to his 'Ode to Britain', where he describes Sierra Leone as 'the country to which many of my countrymen owe their freedom and liberty of conscience.'

Diplomatically, he makes no reference to the involvement of Britain in the slave trade from the mid-seventeenth century onwards: from 1795 to 1804 alone, it is estimated that some

400,000 slaves were taken from Africa by ships operating out of British ports, before slavery was outlawed in the British Empire three years later. What is interesting is that Selim, as a former slave, should find himself involved in several situations which were closely related to this issue, such as Baikie's expedition up the Niger, which was ostensibly to establish mission and trading stations to displace slavery, while Burton's appointment to Fernando Po, although he himself might have questioned this, was primarily to exercise British influence in preventing the continuing trade in slaves. Finally, it is ironic that Selim should apparently be caught up in the local wars which blighted the attempts of the freed slaves from the USA to establish their colony in Liberia.

My account of Selim's life is largely taken from his own narrative and the remarks of others such as Burton; in general very little has been added to provide background other than, for example, the chapter on Muslim slavery and the conditions of nineteenth-century tropical travel. There are accurate contemporary accounts of estate life and a wealth of information on the conditions of workers in Scotland's north-east countryside which have been included to contrast with Selim's own relatively comfortable life there and the circumstances of his native village. There is one exception where I have taken the liberty of hypothesising Selim's experience. This relates to his time at Murtle, where the only strictly factual material available is the Thurburn family history and the physical attributes of Murtle House and estate, together with the census records providing, in addition to the family, the names of the servants and guests at the time.

The celebration at Murtle of Anna Thurburn's wedding in 1849 is an example: the wedding did take place at this time, but the details of the servants' ball are conjectural, although Anna did present a bouquet to the young Queen Victoria on her way to Balmoral.[6] The justification for this departure from the approach taken in the remainder of this work is simply that there would hardly have been a story to tell if the most important period in Selim's development had rested simply on his dedication to his patron; he appears to have written nothing else on his time there.

Apart from its personal interest, Selim's story may be of some historical significance. There are numerous accounts by former slaves taken from West Africa to the American plantations, but to this author's knowledge, none from East or North Africa where the trade, in a Muslim context, was based on very different premises. Certainly there appears to be nothing in English. Nor is there any record of a European having penetrated the Nuba Mountains by the 1830s, although the Bohemian traveller Ignaz Pallme, seeking a possible trade route into Central Africa, got close in 1837–38, but was prevented from entering Taqali itself. He did have extended conversations in El Obeid with a prince of Taqali, who may have been one of the three princes of that territory referred to by Selim. Selim's early recollections of his life there, its economy and customs, is therefore a valuable addition to our knowledge of one of the most fascinating societies in Africa at this time, not least because of its lineage as a so-called 'Muslim' kingdom straddling Arabic and Black African cultures. The most comprehensive background to this kingdom from earliest times is provided by Professor Janet Ewald in her scholarly study *Soldiers, Traders, and Slaves: State Formation and Economic Transformation in the Greater Nile Valley, 1700–1885*, although she was apparently unaware of Selim's account.

The inclusion of the extended description of Taqali and its

customs might be questioned in a work which is intended to focus on Selim's life, but the records in the first third of the nineteenth century are scant and Selim's own description is a very valuable account. (The great German explorer, Gustav Nachtigal, despite his extensive travels in the Sudan in the 1870s, did not penetrate south of El Obeid in Kordofan.) Taqali lies on the extremity of the Nuba Mountains, a region which, because of its remoteness and relative inaccessibility, combined with its unique customs and variety of languages, attracted considerable anthropological interest in the twentieth century.

The fact remains that the Nuba Mountains and its peoples are unique, and within that, Taqali itself, in its history and traditions, is quite distinctive. Among the great variety of spellings for this area, I have adopted that used by Ewald, although there is now no district of that name, only a town called Tagali. Selim himself calls it 'Tegeley'. Despite a semblance of peace in the Nuba Mountains, following agreements between the Sudan People's Liberation Army and the official Government of Sudan, the war which raged from 1985 onwards has left its considerable scars and the future autonomy of the region is by no means guaranteed.

There are obviously many gaps in Selim's story, in particular his travels with John Thurburn in the late 1840s and in the years after leaving Richard Burton's services in 1864 up to Selim's reported death in Liberia in 1875. It would be especially satisfying if some of these gaps could be even partially filled and I would be more than pleased to receive any relevant information which might amplify this biography in any future edition.

CHAPTER ONE
The Kingdom of Taqali

Untam'd, untaught, in arts and arms unskill'd,
Their patrimonial soil they rudely till'd,
Shelter'd in lowly huts their fragile forms
From burning suns and desolating storms.
See the boy bounding through the eager race;
The fierce youth, shouting foremost in the chase,
Drives the grim lion from his ancient woods.

SELIM'S VILLAGE LAY on a fertile plateau on the north-eastern side of the Nuba Mountains, about 150km due west of the Nile, now known as South Kordofan. It is dominated by great granite domes rising 500–1,000 metres above the surrounding plains. The mountains are sometimes in long ranges, or otherwise occur as isolated massifs or even single crags. The Nuba Mountain area covers approximately 78,000 square kilometres or about the same area as Scotland, of which Taqali occupies a relatively small portion in the extreme north-east of these ranges. In Selim's day the surrounding foothills were covered with dense woodland dissected by steep rocky ravines and tumbling mountain streams which led to the moist grasslands in the plains below.

An attractive, well-watered country, its hard-working people cultivated a wide range of crops, including millet, sesame, maize, black corn, groundnuts and beans. They kept pigs, cattle and camels, but their principal livestock were sheep and goats. They were a settled agricultural people, in contrast to the pastoral and nomadic Baqqara of Arab origin, who wandered across the plains below: it has been suggested that the incursions of these cattle herders was an important factor in driving the Nuba into the mountains. The Nuba farmers cultivated both 'near farms' in small plots, often by ingenious terracing and irrigation, and larger 'far farms' on the more extensive clay plains below. Selim gives a good picture of his country:

> It is an undulating table-land, bounded by two ranges of low hills, the highest part of which may be about 3,000 to 4,000 feet; and in the centre is a watercourse, flowing through the whole distance, some 16 miles, parallel with the Nile, south to north to the lower part of the valley. Dry in the dry seasons, during the rains it is a complete

> torrent, running some seven or eight knots, and in many places very deep and perfectly impassable. On either side of this mountain-stream the country is all under cultivation; in short, the site is so thickly peopled that many of the inhabitants are compelled to make farms 4 or 5 miles beyond the principality. The ground which my father possessed there was not sufficient for the growth of corn for all our family; he therefore obtained a grant of land in the territory of a prince of the name of Daldoum Abshenet; and it was there that the greater part of our supplies were produced and there also that the intended farm for your humble servant was cleared and made ready for him… the valley, as far as I can remember, was very productive, the waving corn growing luxuriantly throughout all parts of it, and cotton was cultivated for the manufacture of country clothes.[1]

These clothes consisted, for the richer inhabitants, of a long gown reaching down to the ankles, with wide loose sleeves. Lower on the social scale, the dress would simply be a cotton blanket, kilted at the waist and with the spare cloth tied over one shoulder. Until the 1950s, many of the mountain Nuba to the south went virtually naked – after bathing, people considered themselves 'undressed' if they had not smeared their bodies with butter, warmed in the sun. Others might use an ointment composed of bone marrow, cloves and sandalwood oils. With no currency, the whole economy was based on barter; the sandal-makers and weavers, for example, would trade their products for food. Taxes were usually paid in the form of service to the prince. As in many other parts of Africa, in order to preserve the flocks, animals were rarely killed for meat; goat's milk and butter were important items of diet. Selim describes the relatively primitive agriculture, the plough:

> being a long pole, with something similar to a shovel attached to the end of it. With this instrument the surface of the ground is broken, after which the seed (consisting of Indian corn and maize) is sown in small quantities at certain distances from each other. After it has grown a certain length, part of it is transplanted into different fields, thus giving the crop full scope and encouragement to grow. When the corn begins to change colour, the rainy season declines, till at length the refulgent rays of the sun perceive the inhabitant of the vale preparing to reap his harvest. The rain is over, the dry season is on; many begin to reap the fruits of their labour. The day of shearing is generally ended with dancing, of which amusement they are very fond. The reader, perhaps, will inquire what sort of drink these dancers use? His mind will very likely answer, Jamaica rum, French brandy, or Irish whisky. But no, water is their chief drink. They have a thick intoxicating liquor, which they make from the Indian corn; but such a luxury is only used on extraordinary occasions. After all their harvest festivities are over, they give themselves up to all the indolent habits prevalent in these eastern countries; and lounge in their booths until the appearance of the skies proclaim the distant approach of the rainy season.[2]

The origins of the Muslim kingdom of Taqali are disputed. Legend has it that it started with the marriage of a Ja'ali holy man, a descendent of the Prophet's uncle from old Upper Nubia, who settled in Taqali around 1530 with a princess from the Nuba

Mountains. From this time, a long continuous line of Muslim kings ruled the territory. Modern scholarship suggests that the kingdom is of much more recent origin, although it is known that it had been nominally a subject state of the Funj Kingdom of Sennar to the east, a black sultanate of fabulous wealth and power based on gold and slaves, which had ruled a great area of the Sudan between the sixteenth and nineteenth centuries.[3] Often described as a Muslim kingdom, the inhabitants of Taqali nevertheless appear to have been largely animist, ie worshipped natural spirits, although still following some Muslim customs. It is said that Taqali kings adhered to Islam to create a sanctuary from slave raiding, which they themselves indulged in.[4]

According to Selim, he 'never observed any of the ceremonies of the Moslem faith in my country, and as the people are taught to believe in the existence of the soul hereafter, and as I never saw any idols or other heathen superstitions in the valley of Tegeley, I may infer, from our proximity to Abyssinia, that the religion is a corrupted form of Christianity.'[5] Selim contradicts his assertion on the absence of Muslim ceremony by saying that circumcision was practised, as was fasting for a month during the daylight hours, no doubt for the period of Ramadan. On circumcision, he records a custom whereby:

> about a month after the ceremony of circumcision, a number of young men convene at the house where the rite had been performed, and sally from thence through the country on hunting excursions. Everything falls a prey to the hunter's knife and spear; and on these occasions the poultry-yard suffers most, while the poor owners are mere lookers on at these depredations, it being deemed sacred [sic] to interfere with the behaviour of these young men. [6]

Selim himself was not a Muslim (he records an unsuccessful conversion attempt on his journey down the Nile), although the kingdom of Taqali, sometimes described as the 'cradle of Islam', was more influenced by Muslim culture than anywhere else in the Nuba Mountains. This would certainly accord with its position on the north-east extremity of this massif, more accessible to penetration from the Muslim north.[7]

In her study of the history of Taqali, Professor Janet Ewald suggests that the people were Nuba highlanders long before becoming subjects of the Muslim kings, and continued to be so after the rise of these kings from the mid-eighteenth century.[8] It has been said that there are as many Nuba languages as there are hills, such is the variety of culture across this district, which it has been claimed had more linguistic diversity than the whole of Africa south of the equator. The people of Taqali, despite their Muslim overlordship, continued to practise local religions and to follow local animist leaders.[9] The adoption of Islam may have been used as a means to achieve higher social status, community leaders accepting Islam to form an 'aristocracy'. The other Nuba highlanders certainly kept pigs and ate pork, and the indications are that they were less influenced by Muslim practice than people in Taqali; however, they paid tribute to the kings of Taqali, usually in the form of slaves; initially they did not put great value on gold, which they carried in ostrich feather quills.[10]

In Taqali, as elsewhere in the Nuba Mountains, power appears to have been shared between female spirit mediums and male leaders, kings and princes, who were also *kujurs*, or shamans, and practised ancestor spirit worship.[11] The king would take part in the installation of a new medium, who would be the head of a hierarchy of mediums. Female mediums foretold events, and male leaders paid close attention to their prophecies.

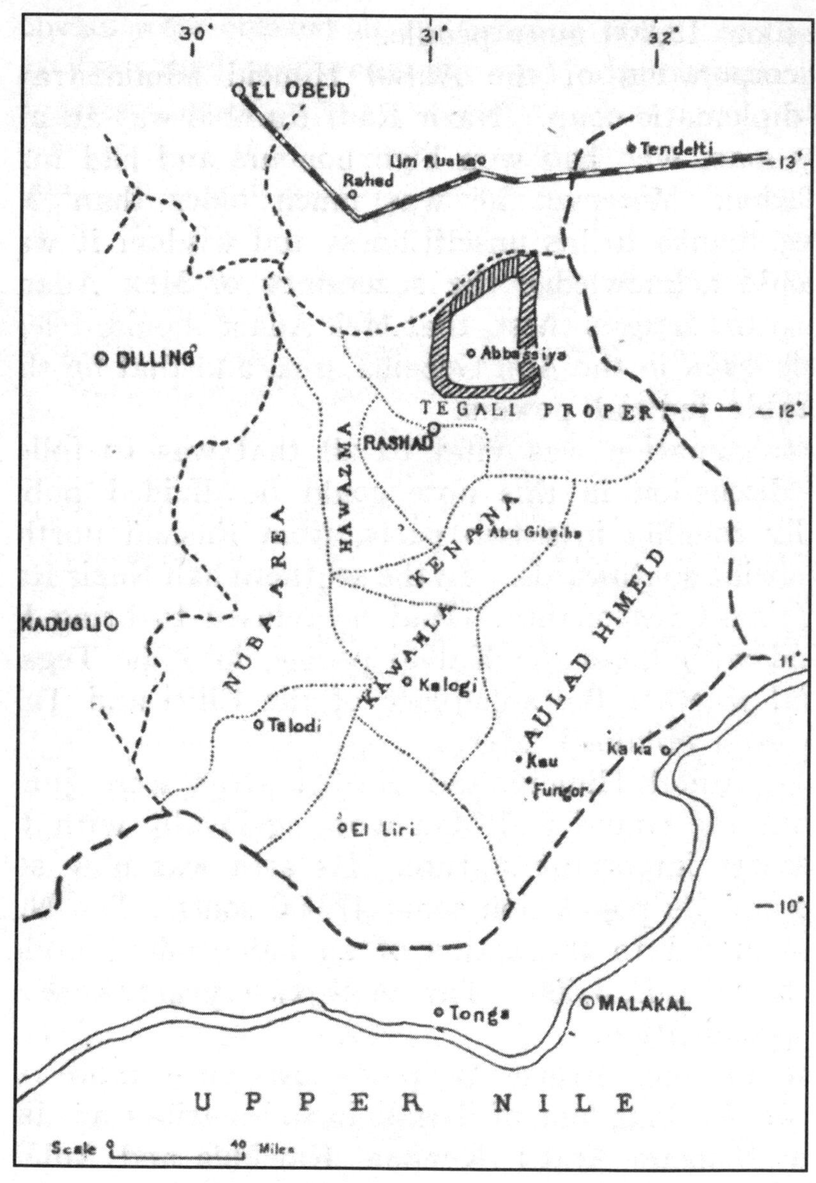

Location of Taqali in the Nuba mountains
(Trustees of the National Library of Scotland)

The mediums also administered oaths, helped to settle disputes and, protected by their ritual spears, acted as envoys in battles between tribes.[12] Among the most important ceremonies were the rain sacrifices conducted at sacred places or shrines, said to involve young girls chosen by the king.

The royal stronghold was at Tasi,[13] at the base of the most northerly of three steep, sugar loaf hills, commanding an extensive view overlooking the wide green valley of Taqali to the granite range of Kejakja beyond.[14] Here the *maak*, or king, kept his harem of 300 concubines in a stone building on the summit of a rock, a fortress with only one means of access. The *maak* was both a mediator and a warrior, controlling access to military resources, especially the relatively few horses in the kingdom and a large number of slaves.[15] A description around the time of Selim's capture indicates the king's function:

> The diwan in which he [the *maak*] holds his audience is a large salon, built of stone, decorated with swords, spears, and other warlike trophies. Eighteen or twenty of his bodyguard are always present. They sit armed with spears, and form a kind of living fence. The sultan proceeds every morning with sunrise immediately after prayers into the divan, hears all causes himself, and issues his decision immediately.[16]

At its height, this independent kingdom held sway over 50,000 square kilometres, from Khor Abu Habl ('el Nil') in the north to Talodi in the south, and controlled the fabled gold mines of Sheibun and Mandi. However, the area of Taqali proper was probably not more that 250 square kilometres. Elles, writing in the 1930s, describes the topography of the country:

> An attractive country… the gently rounded slopes of the foothills form a restful contrast to the upflung masses of naked granite which crown the higher summits to the west. The green smoothness of thickly wooded hillsides is pleasantly broken by broad valleys, steep glens and narrow ravines, while here and there a patch of cultivation provides vivid colour to attract the eye… streams everywhere, tumbling over smooth-worn rocks into deep inviting pools, join to flood the sandy khors in the plains below… to the north and east, the hills drop abruptly to the plain, which stretches away northwards… fertile valleys lead down from the hills into this plain, extending into rich low-lying nilas which afford water and grazing to herds of cattle and camels in the dry season.[17]

Selim describes how, at the end of the harvest, the local prince, wearing robes of the brightest colours he could find, ordered a great assembly of the people. After addressing them about the prospects for the year, he rode out of the palace, galloping a distance of two miles to the centre of the main river. All the men of the village, dressed as for war, followed him, shouting and dancing. Calling out the prince's name and making the death yell in their loudest voices, they hunted down a goat to sacrifice. Whoever found a goat first, ran with it to the prince and cut its throat underneath the belly of his horse. He then gave some of the blood in his hands for the prince to sprinkle himself with and then everyone else followed suit. Other festivals known as *Sibirs* (to encourage animal fertility or to celebrate harvests) were enjoyed, taking different forms according to tribe.

The people themselves were intelligent, handsome and well built, and despite their reputation as ferocious warriors, one

European missionary, Fr Stanislao Carceri, claimed, 'if they see a stranger trusts them, and if they have no fear of him, they are the most pacific, hospitable people in the world.'[18] He also described them as frank, sincere, cheerful and very intelligent. They were reputed to be much more industrious than other tribes in Kordofan,[19] and even in modern times were said to be particularly receptive to education and improvements in agriculture and veterinary services.[20] In Selim's time, they were reckoned to be considerably more advanced than the surrounding hill tribes, and were proud to be identified with their unique kingdom. They traded freely with Arab traders ('*jellaba*'), in gold, ostrich feathers, ivory and, above all, in slaves.

The part of Taqali where Selim had his home was ruled by the despotic Prince Chammaroo, who had the power of life or death over his people, and at whose court Selim's uncle was feted as a heroic warrior: he had killed a lion single-handed. He led a raid in retaliation against a gang of robbers which had been ravaging the district; one of the women caught up in the exchange of hostages was Selim's grandmother:

> [Selim's uncle] was presented to Prince Chammaroo, who at once gave him the command of an expedition against a predatory horde that infested the neighbourhood of the country. My father and nearly the whole of the able-bodied men in the house at once volunteered to accompany the lion-killer, and after four days' march into some country to the eastward, that is to say towards Sennar, they came upon the robbers just at dusk, and completely routed them, taking possession of everything that the enemy had, besides bringing in four prisoners. The implements used in Tegeley warfare are spears and shields; and I never

> remember having seen a gun until I came to the camp of the Egyptian soldiers, between three and four days' journey from my country. The captives taken in the affray were shortly afterwards ransomed, and the mother of the chief of the enemy was sent to us, as a guarantee for the future amicable relations of the two tribes, my grandmother being sent as a hostage to the enemy's country in exchange.[21]

As the favoured elder son, Selim had the promise of a farm from his father, who owned two small villages of well-built huts set into the hillside. The architecture, unique to Taqali, was relatively sophisticated compared to other parts of Africa: each round room in the houses was built about ten metres from each other, the floors being of stones and mud. Four or five such rooms were commonly surrounded by a wall almost two metres high, leaving a central courtyard with two entrances. The courtyard was used for sleeping during the hottest part of the year. Selim's father's house comprised two bedrooms, a kitchen, a mill room and a goat fold.

Despite all precautions, predatory animals did sometimes invade. One of Prince Chammaroo's children had been attacked by a lion within the royal courtyard, leaving her permanently half-scalped.

Selim became a lord-in-waiting to the prince's children, while his elder sister acted as nurse to them. He had prospects of becoming a personage of some importance in his community, with land, crops and cattle. He was later to recall his jealousy of his younger brother, who had usurped his place at his mother's breast – she apparently resented her husband's favouring of his eldest son, and Selim was often at the receiving end of her displaced ire:

> I dearly loved my father, who showered upon me such unmistakable signs of paternal affection that his partiality towards me created an ill-feeling against me on the part of my mother. Her conjugal regard for my father was not of the highest stamp, so that I frequently came in for a scolding intended for my father, and frequently a slapping for myself.[22]

Other than this, the young Selim appears to have had a relatively idyllic life in an area blessed with abundant water and an equable climate, with soils capable of supporting a wide range of food crops, tobacco, and cotton. Selim looked forward to the time when he would leave the herding of his father's flocks to his younger brother and become a proprietor in his own right, a man of substance with a wife and family.

In Taqali, it was usual for husband and wife to be betrothed as children. Only later, when the prospective husband had a home, would he receive his bride. According to Selim, very few of the men took more than one wife. When he reached the age of eight, his father chose what he hoped would be his son's future wife and told Selim what he should do. Custom required Selim to go to her family's house, call the girl by name, and order her to cook for him and come and live in his house. It was customary for the future bride to carry the dishes she had cooked to the house of her betrothed, and, kneeling down before him, await his approval of the food. Acceptance constituted marriage from that day onwards. Young Selim was apparently highly alarmed at the prospect. She was twelve, which alone terrified him. He quietly suggested to the girl that she beat him to show her disapproval. However, her parents received him courteously and indicated that they were not averse to the match.

Children were encouraged to work and become independent from a very early age. Sometimes Selim would be sent to the far fields to scare birds away from the ripening crops. At this time, he had left the court to herd his father's animals; every morning at sunrise he would open the sheep-fold to let out the sheep and goats. One old ram used to lead the way while Selim rode another in the rear. He usually met up with two young herds from neighbouring villages. They had an arrangement to mix their flocks together so that they could share shepherding. In the evening each called his own animals, which readily separated into their respective flocks to return to their folds.

Wildlife was abundant, both in the forests and on the open savannah.[23] Elephants were plentiful in the district until the late nineteenth century. One method of hunting was for a horseman to goad the elephant from the front and, while its attention was distracted, another horseman would dismount and cut its hamstrings from the rear. The elephant, attempting to charge at the front rider, would collapse from its wounds.[24] As late as the 1930s, great game hunts were conducted, when the able-bodied men of Taqali would drive animals from far and near into a narrow defile where they were trapped and killed. A large shady tree would be selected at the foot of the pass that leads down from the royal palace at Tasi for the king's direction of the hunt, and the hunting and feasting would continue for a week.[25]

On one occasion, Selim, whose father had made him a spear and shield like the other warriors, went out with a hunting party on the lookout for anything they could get. One can imagine that the boy could not have been prouder, marching along, his short legs trying to keep pace with these formidable spearmen. Their leader was a grizzled old veteran of many such hunts, who would stop at intervals, signalling silently to the others in the party to crouch down as he sniffed the wind and scanned the horizon. Emerging quietly from thick thornbush into a broad open valley with scattered trees, they were astonished to see a large group of giraffes, quite unaware of the crouching hunters. They had never seen so many together. Selim gives a wonderful evocation of the scene:

> Without the least exaggeration, there must have been at least 200 of these swan-necked and most graceful animals scattered over a vast expanse of the woods below us; and nothing could have added greater novelty to the scene, than a view of our game nibbling, with mouths like the gazelles, the topmost branches of the extensive bush.[26]

Selim's uncle gave the order to split into two groups: one, with Selim among them, to cover the rear of the giraffes and the other to head them off from the front in a wide circling movement. They selected the beast less likely to outrun them and cut it off, knowing it would attempt to double back to rejoin the herd. It was a manoeuvre they had practised many times, but it did not always succeed. Selim's account of this hunt does not reveal the emotions it aroused in him. However, it is not difficult to imagine how his heart must have pounded as he took up his place with his uncle and started moving towards the giraffes, gripping his shield and spear tightly, watching his feet to ensure he did not tread on brittle twigs which would sound the alarm. After what seemed like an eternity, he would have heard a chorus of yells as the warriors in the forward party launched their spears into the flanks of a giraffe, which started running back in the direction of Selim's group. He would have caught a terrifying glimpse of a mottled shape charging through the undergrowth, before his own party rushed forward to unleash their quota of spears into the side of the doomed animal, which collapsed in a clearing about a hundred yards ahead. Selim might have been in time to see the lead hunter draw his knife swiftly across the giraffe's lower neck. Following the kill, everyone danced around, yelling and shouting in exultation, leaping onto the animal to carve out chunks of meat, setting aside the choicer innards to present to the chief.

On their return to the village, the forward party encountered two kidnappers waiting to pounce on lone villagers or unprotected children returning from outlying farms:

> These kidnappers are common throughout the country. They are the off-scourings of the people round about the valley of Tegeley [Taqali] and being of debauched and idle propensities, employ themselves in covertly catching strays, and in selling them to the slave dealers.

Although the hunting party immediately let fly with their spears, the thick forest deflected them and the villains easily escaped into the bush.[27] Even then, the day was not yet done. The other half of the hunting party had killed a fine old lion, but Selim does not elaborate on how this was achieved. However, Pallme describes in some detail the method of a lion hunt in this district. A hunter would creep stealthily forward until he was within a stone's throw of a sleeping lion and select a tree with a suitable fork about fifteen feet above the ground, well beyond the lion's ability to climb. Settling himself carefully in the fork, he would throw a pebble towards the lion, which might barely open his eyes: the second pebble might hit him squarely in the face and he would roar. The hunter would call to him and the lion would move angrily towards the source of the noise.

It would not take him long to spot the hunter and the last few yards would be covered at speed, encountering a barrage of pebbles. Then the first of the hunter's spears would be thrown with maximum force from above. Wounded, the beast would retreat into a nearby bush. But another fusillade of pebbles would rouse him again to attack his tormentor, with the same result, except that he would take more spear thrusts. This time he might not regain the shelter of the bush, which would be the signal for the other watching hunters to rush forward, throwing their remaining spears into the dying animal. Later, the carcase would be bartered with a neighbouring tribe for corn, since the Taqali villagers, by custom, were forbidden to eat the flesh of a lion.[28]

All adult Taqali males were warriors and each was expected to kill a lion at some time. They also took their share in house-building and raising crops. Selim records warfare as a major occupation, including the capture of slaves, which enabled the warrior to purchase his bride. Here, as elsewhere in the Sudan, slave-raiding had gone on since earliest times, and in Selim's boyhood and subsequently, the Nuba Hills were the target for many such raids.

The main threat came from Turco-Egyptian soldiers attacking the villages in organised military expeditions. The villagers' main weapon was their remoteness and their defensible positions on the steep mountainsides. They could launch effective counter-attacks on marauders, who were only too well aware of both their courage and skill with their spears – in Selim's time, there were no guns in Taqali. However, the Nubans were masters of guerrilla warfare, retreating in the face of determined attacks to their impregnable mountain strongholds, but replying with very effective surprise counter-attacks.

To maintain their fighting prowess, wrestling matches were features of the culture of the Nuba Mountains, including ferocious stick fighting and bloody arm wrestling with sharpened bracelets, now banned. It is curious that Selim makes no mention of such contests; possibly they were not a feature of life in Taqali itself.

Nothing in Selim's account of his early years contradicts other sources of information on his home district and its life, apart from minor inconsistencies – at one point he declares that his community subsisted on maize, but he also says many other food crops were grown. Given the plurality of religious practice in Taqali, with traditional customs thriving alongside Muslim rites, it is perhaps not surprising that Selim's references to religion are ambiguous. His record of 1846 was written some ten years after his arrival in Scotland, when memory might have been affected by the many novel experiences he had had since his boyhood in the Sudan. He does apologise for the lack of geographical detail given in his memoir, attributing this to his youth at the time of his capture. In his preface he describes Africa as the 'least known' quarter of the globe: 'Ignorance, barbarity, and superstition prevail in its centre, and the unhealthy nature of its climate renders it almost impracticable for any European to travel into.'[29] He was not to know that his travels with Burton in West Africa fifteen years later would amply confirm all of these attributes of the so-called 'Dark Continent', which despite the efforts of intrepid explorers, still had large gaps in its known geography.

CHAPTER TWO

'A thing to be bartered for'

The smoking village vanished from the plain,
The strong were captur'd, and the feeble slain.
Far thence the ruthless spoiler dragg'd his prey,
Condemn'd to distant climes and foreign sway
...
Rough was the path the weary wand'rers trac'd,
O'er burning sands, a bare unwater'd waste...

THE CAPTURE WAS swift and ruthless. Over the brow of the hill loped two black-bearded Arabs, their dusty *jellabas* flapping round their ankles in the dry desert wind. All around Selim, his goats and sheep were bleating intermittently and tugging at the coarse grass of the valley floor. He was not concerned when one of the men, in an accent unfamiliar to him, asked if he had any goats for purchase – this was not an unusual request. The eight-year-old answered 'No, sir,' but the words were hardly spoken before the taller of the two reached forward, grasped him by the hand and started pulling. The boy fell to the ground, yelling for his father and mother. But there was little chance that anyone would hear him in this deserted valley far from his village. The sun was already setting. The more he screamed and twisted his body, the tighter became the grip on his thin wrists. He was being dragged through the thornbush. Escape was impossible.

The shorter of the two slavers took a dagger from his belt, cut a green switch from one of these bushes and proceeded to whip Selim's legs and thighs – he was naked, as were all the young herdsmen in this part of the Nuba Mountains. The pain was severe. Rivulets of blood ran down his calves. Resistance only increased the severity of the whipping, and Selim's protestations were soon reduced to a tearful whimper as he was forced into a fast trot across the plain by the now silent men. Late at night, they reached a farmhouse, where, given no food or drink, he was bound hand and foot and laid on the bare ground. He wept uncontrollably throughout that long night:

> I was now a slave beyond doubt. From being a companion of princes, I had dwindled into a thing to be bartered for, to be bought, to be sold at the pleasure of another man. My dear father was far away from me, and I had no relative

> or friends to sympathise with me in my luckless destiny… my eyes have never since fallen upon parent, family, or friend of my youth.[1]

On the morning after his capture, one of the slavers, armed with a ferocious hippopotamus-hide whip and with a sword slung over his shoulder, marched him for several hours to the large Arab village of Tegla. After interminable bargaining in Arabic, which Selim could not understand, he was sold to the chief. But here in Tegla he was astonished to encounter a girl, Medina, whom he knew from Prince Chammaroo's court. They fell upon each other's necks and wept both in sorrow and relief at finding one another. Medina's tale was a dismal one of intrigue and duplicity on the part of the prince and his courtiers. Her brother, a powerful chief in his own right, had refused to allow her to become part of the prince's harem. Chammaroo then arranged for Medina to be sent on an errand, with instructions for her to be waylaid by some of the prince's emissaries and sold to the Arab chief. She warned Selim to do exactly as he was told by his new master, as killing them both would not worry the Arab in the least.

They were secured together, with iron chains riveted on her right leg, and then locked with a key to Selim's left. A strict watch was set over them. Medina was always making plans for their escape and one night Selim succeeded in forcing the chains off his feet, but she, after desperate attempts to follow suit, did not succeed; in any case, both were terrified at the thought of recapture and punishment, which might have included execution *pour décourager les autres*. Not long afterwards, the chief joined a caravan of merchants and travelled with them to a village where he hoped to sell his captives. The journey took a whole day and

Enslavement

by the time they arrived the market had broken up. He failed to get a single bid and was obliged to return. Selim and Medina were dismayed to learn that friends from their own village had been searching for them but had been told that they had already been taken to a distant land.

Several days later, Selim was woken long before dawn to start his journey with a large caravan heading northwards. For the first day, he and Medina trudged over a barren landscape of sand, a few outcropping rocks and the occasional baobab tree. They had never before seen such a featureless plain, without a single habitation. As with other travellers before and after him, Selim was plagued by a notorious plant, which is well described by Michael Asher, who has made several journeys across the Sahara in modern times:

> I suddenly found myself covered in viciously sharp thistles, which embedded themselves in my arms, legs and face. The faster I tried to extract them, the more they stuck: they worked themselves inside my trousers, up the sleeves of my shirt and even into my lips and ears. It was my first experience of heskaniit grass, the desert traveller's nightmare.[2]

At nightfall, the tents were pitched beside a well which was made from the hollowed out centre of a baobab, the water fresh but with the musky smell of the tree bark. The second day was even longer, the country entirely bare and eroded, with huge desiccated cracks and crevasses; they marched on after nightfall to reach the village of Albeit (likely to be the modern Al Bahr al Abyad, about 35km north-west of Kosti). Here they encountered the Baqqara, Arabic-speaking Muslim herders, whose appearance astonished Selim. They wore rings in their nostrils and ears and rode decorated bullocks.

Despite the traditional enmity between these fierce pastoralists and the settled inhabitants of Taqali, the caravan was hospitably received by the Baqqara, who, even among themselves, seemed to be in a state of continual warfare. At a nearby Turkish military camp established for carrying out slave hunts, slaves were examined minutely from their teeth to their toes. On the following day they resumed their trek to El Obeid with both the Turks and their own master. Selim was dismayed to see the other slaves attached to camels by forked sticks and a number of young girl captives being forced by the Turkish soldiers to mount their dromedaries.

Four days later they reached El Obeid, the sprawling capital of Kordofan and the most important garrison town of the Turco-Egyptian army in the Sudan. It was also a place of pilgrimage and an important junction for several ancient slaving and trade routes – a major staging post on the routes to fabled Sennar, capital of the Funj kingdom east of the White Nile, and to the gold and slave market of Sheibun south of the Nuba Mountains (later to be the first target of the Mahdist uprising in the 1880s). At the time of Selim's enslavement, Kordofan had largely been brought under Egyptian control – the 'Turkiyya' – by Muhammed Ali, Viceroy of Egypt, which was under the jurisdiction of the Ottoman Empire. It was Muhammed who had suppressed the peoples of Darfur and Kordofan after the battle of Bara in 1821 and made his son-in-law, the notorious Khusraw el Dermali, governor ('defturdar') of these provinces. The town contained a garrison of some 3,000 infantrymen and 2,000 cavalrymen, in addition to a civilian population of about 20,000.[3] The garrison's whole purpose was to subjugate the region and to aid the governor in exploiting its resources, mainly in the form of slaves, ivory and gold, and to plunder its wealth.

El Obeid was really a collection of villages, each with its own distinctive populations: one housed people from Darfur to the west who had decided to settle there, another was for the pilgrims passing through, while the large Turkish military camp held the main government offices, officers' quarters, barracks and bazaar.[4] After the battle of Bara, the Turks had destroyed the original

Slave raiders (Michael Russell Publishing Ltd)

town. It now presented a dismal prospect of huts built of straw, with a few of clay, that Selim could only compare unfavourably with his own well-constructed hill village. Millet was grown round the huts, which could barely be seen above the crop. When the rains came, flash floods created an impassable muddy quagmire, cutting off the village until they receded. An inescapable feature of El Obeid was the sight and smell of death. Innumerable bones, both human and animal – horses, donkeys, camels – littered the ground between the huts, no one apparently thinking it worth the trouble to bury them. The traveller Pallme noted:

> as soon as a slave dies, a rope is bound round his foot, by which he is dragged out of the hut with as little ceremony as a dead beast, and scraped into the sand anywhere, or even left to decompose in the grass until the hyenas come to gnaw his bones in the night; the remains are devoured in the morning by the dogs, two or more of which may not infrequently be seen fighting over a human arm or foot.[5]

Selim now began to imagine 'that he had arrived amongst the people that lived at the end of the world, and whose business it is to kill all the blacks, and to use their blood as a dye for red cloth'. To him, the sight of 'many of the soldiers wearing scarlet caps' only confirmed his fear and he gave himself up for lost, 'trepidation and despair seized our souls and bodies'.[6]

When the millet was harvested the aftermath of herbage was burnt, creating dense clouds of smoke and releasing innumerable locusts which the locals fell upon greedily to eat raw – another sight which amazed the young captives. The souk was open daily for the sale of camels, cows, sheep, goats, and asses, sour milk, butter, lard, garden and wild fruits, firewood and grasses. More often than not, an auction of items, such as old clothes, would be held, with the crier marching through the milling throng, yelling for bids. As Pallme observed, the same process was followed for the sale of humans:

> The unfortunate being offered for sale is led about like any other commodity by the crier, who expatiates upon the beauty, or other characteristics of the slave, and walking before him, bawls out the price. If a purchaser present himself, he enters upon an examination of his fellow creature, as we should examine a head of cattle in Europe; he looks at his teeth, eyes, hands, and feet, and enquires into his age, place of birth, and in short into every circumstance which might influence his price, while the unfortunate wretch follows the crier like a dog, anxiously awaiting his future fate. A mother may not be separated by the infant at her breast, but children of three or four years may be disposed of separately; the latter are very reasonable; their price varies from only thirty to sixty

piastres [eight shillings and sixpence to seventeen shillings]. Full grown slaves fluctuate according to the supply of the market; girls and boys from ten to fifteen years of age are in the greatest request, and cost from one hundred to three hundred piasters; if there be few for sale, and many Djelabi are about to travel to Cairo, the price, of course, rises. There are certain conditions under which a slave may be returned to the vendor, eg if he have offensive breath, or snore in his sleep, or be troubled with incontinence of urine, or for any one of these vices he may be sent back at the expiration of the third day; should a female slave be pregnant, the term is somewhat prolonged. The slave trade is not always carried on in retail, for the Djelabi buy slaves in lots; on these occasions, however, the individuals are singly examined, and the aged and infirm are separated from the flock. The chief object is to have as many young girls and boys in a lot, and to be able to transport them safely to Egypt; thus every one in purchasing, looks chiefly to their age, and a boy or girl, beyond the thirteenth or fifteenth year, is seldom sold in the bazaar of Cairo or Alexandria; every one, in fact, prefers bringing them up according to his own taste, and for this purpose select the youngest.[7]

Arthur T Holroyd, the author of *Egypt and Mahomed Ali Pasha* (1837), is quoted extensively by the diplomat Sir John Bowring in the latter's important *Report on Egypt 1823–1838*, where he says:

almost every person in Kordofan is a slave merchant and if an individual can gain only a few piastres by the sale, the unfortunate captive is sure to change hands. I hardly

> ever entered a house in El Obeid without noticing one or more slaves in irons.[8]

In El Obeid Selim and Medina were sold to another Arab. Subsequently, with no little bitterness, they saw their previous captor and some of his Taqali friends mounted on the finest Arab horses, which Selim assumed had been bought with the proceeds of their own sale. Watching this caravan departing for Taqali, Medina broke down in floods of tears, calling out piteously the names of her brother, her relatives and all the close friends she had known at home. She and Selim realised that they were now forever severed from their homeland, and they wailed for all that they had known, all that they would never see again. Their situation was not improved when, a few days later, they were sold to a Turkish captain (or *agha*) in the Egyptian army. He was tyrannical in the extreme. Medina was immediately made a member of his *seraglio,* while Selim became a general servant, at the beck and call of the captain and his visitors. The captain treated soldiers and civilians alike – brutally. Selim describes in detail the horrendous beating given to a camel driver:

> It appears that the miserable wretch was four days behind time; the moment therefore that the Agha heard his name, he jumped up in a rage, and calling the man by certain most unseemly names, ordered him to receive fifty strokes with a large cudgel kept for the purpose. The wretch groaned a death-like moan; he was thrown on his side and the bastinado was administered upon his shoulders. When ordered up after the castigation, his body was bleeding in different parts, and his cheek was skinned by the convulsive efforts with which he raised his head and struck his cheek

> on the ground after every blow. This was the way that the Agha answered every complaint that was brought to him, soldiers suffered, civilians groaned under the lash, and every attempt at begging pardon was answered only by a double flagellation.[9]

He himself was required to answer the captain's call, irrespective of the distance:

> my master was sure to be heard crying my name a quarter of a mile's distance from the house, at which I had to run out to meet him and carry his sword home. These, and other sufferings of the like nature, prepared me for my subsequent career, and fitted me for the journey on the desert.[10]

One day, having been sent on an errand by the head lady of the *seraglio*, he was called to explain where he had been. The captain then commenced beating Selim in the most vicious fashion all over his body, not excluding his head. Selim became unconscious, with blood running out of his ears. He thereafter suffered some deafness and what he described as 'wheezing in the ears'. On another occasion, Selim served out a few more cups of coffee than required for a houseful of guests; the captain waited till he was asleep, then started to horse-whip him mercilessly. Selim was only saved from death by a higher ranking slave who took the whip from the enraged captain's hand. During the six months Selim served under this monster, Medina was sold to yet another purchaser and the two young slaves lost touch.

CHAPTER THREE
The Nile Journey

Beyond Sahara's wilderness, where heaves
The arid surge, o'erwhelming in its sweep
Horse, horseman, and the camel's towering crest,
As by the stars the struggling caravan,
At midnight hour, their sultry voyage steer.

SELIM'S FORTUNES CHANGED when one day a kindly looking Arab came and took coffee with the captain. Afterwards, Selim was asked to go with the stranger to fetch some soap. The journey seemed endless, though it was taken at a fast pace. As sunset approached, Selim had the temerity to ask how he was going to find his way home but was told not to worry. He was weary to the point of exhaustion when they eventually reached their destination. He was taken to a house where he met two more Arabs, a slave boy and three girls from Darfur, who became his playmates. For the rest of his life, Selim was unsure whether his new master, Jubalee, had cheated the Turkish captain, or whether he had really been sold for soap.

What mattered was that Jubalee was a relatively decent master, which is more than can be said for his Arab companions, Achmet and Mehemmet, apparently natives of New Dongola, a substantial settlement on the Lower Nile. Mehemmet often amused himself by applying the lash to the slaves. As their complement of slaves was now complete with the addition of Selim, the party of Arabs began to make preparations for the long journey down the Nile, the first part of which involved crossing the notorious Bahayuda (Bayuda) Desert between the Blue Nile and White Nile, a ten-day journey. In addition to a horse and an ass, camels were purchased, together with water skins, corn and dates.

Much of the country was composed of dry limestone and sand, with hardly a vestige of plant life, according to Selim, not even a single blade of grass. Subsequently, they went through dense acacia forest, before emerging into the desert proper with its soft orange sand-sheets and scattered trees, then ascending the great dune of Goz ad-Dulu, which taxed both camels and men. Later the sand gave way to vast stony plains with mirages shimmering in the distance. Here they met up with the nomadic Hawawir tribe and their great camel flocks. This was the eastern edge of the Sahara with its rolling sand dunes and ergs, the upflung masses of the great rock inselbergs punctuating the arid landscape. The seasoned Scottish explorer James Grant, who had travelled widely in Africa, Abyssinia and India, said that travel in that region was 'the very worst, from its barrenness, its heat, and from the fatigue and discomfort it necessitates'.[1] The Italian missionary LG Massaia, writing in 1851, emphasised, 'the first care is for the water-bags... for should these fail there is nothing save death', and commented on the emotional effect this landscape had on him: 'the prospect of that vast and arid plain, the immensity of its horizon, the monotonous uniformity, the deep silence that surrounds everything, all have the effect of producing a feeling of profound sadness'.[2]

Selim's caravan was very frugal with water and provisions. As a precaution, the water skins had been divided among the loads, but the main supply was being carried by the spirited grey camel entrusted to Selim's care. One day, an incident occurred which caused them to become agitated in the extreme. A female slave was taking a spell on the saddle, while he sat behind her, holding on to the after-pommel. Under a blazing sun, the string of camels slowly crossed the barren wilderness, the water camel in the rear. There was a dead camel in their path – not an unusual occurrence. In the desert heat, the most appalling odour arose from the corpse. The nostrils of the camels, previously shut to reduce moisture loss, started twitching; the beasts lost composure and started to dance around, thoroughly upset.

Selim slid off the back, and the woman was pitched headlong from the saddle as their camel took off at speed. Total pandemonium ensued. With all the beasts out of control, masters and slaves alike raced after Selim's camel in an effort to save its cargo of water. It kicked and pranced around until the inevitable disaster: all of the skins burst and the precious fluid drained away into the sands of the desert. The next nearest source of fresh water was at the Nile. For five days, which to Selim seemed like fifty, water was doled out in mouthfuls after sunset. No cooking was undertaken; the only food was dry corn and dates.

Everyone raised thanks to Allah when, finally, they reached an oasis and were offered hospitality. Selim describes the sensuous delight of feasting on melons and corn alternately. The following morning, the caravan arrived at the banks of the Nile, where they stopped while Jubalee and Mehemet crossed the river to enjoy Sennar, a great centre for trade in all sorts of commodities including slaves, camels, horses, tamarind fruit, gold dust, tobacco and civet for fixing scent.

> Here we fattened for a fortnight upon the products of the land, Indian corn in any quantity, water-melons, fowls from the neighbouring farms, with occasionally some camel's flesh; and for vegetables the young leaves of the water-melon and the Senna plant – Sennar being the noted spot for that useful medicine.[3]

Shereif Achmet, the old man left in charge of the caravan, appears to have treated the slaves well. One day Selim was sent to collect water from the river. After filling a wooden bowl, he glanced upriver and to his utter astonishment and dismay saw 'an object with a black bottom topped by white sheets coming towards him at speed'.[4] He was momentarily riveted to the spot. The thing, which apparently had eyes, was hurtling straight towards him. With a shriek, Selim threw the bowl from his head, smashing it to pieces on the ground, and ran to the shereif to gasp out his story. What he had seen was a boat, something completely new in his experience. He was severely reprimanded for breaking the bowl and was lucky to escape a flogging.

Sennar was once the centre of a vast kingdom stretching from the Red Sea to the White Nile. The king rode out in great state each week to one of his country houses, accompanied by hundreds of horsemen, women and footmen. By the 1830s it had declined considerably from its previous magnificence. When Mehemet and Jubalee returned after their fortnight's stay there, they brought with them a large number of other merchants and their goods, camels, horses, and armaments, all making up a formidable protected caravan to continue their journey downriver. It would have been an impressive sight: several hundred men and beasts, including camels, donkeys and prancing horses, and a retinue of slaves for sale in the markets of the Lower Nile.

Day after day, they travelled slowly down the river under the direction of a local Arab guide. He left them when they set off across the Libyan desert, as it was then known. This hazardous route cut off one of the great meanders of the Nile, which meant they would probably avoid the attentions of the predatory Shayqiyya.[5] A feature of this desert were the high dunes which had to be crossed; together with the other cameleers, Selim took particular care on the downslopes; especially if the camels were roped together, chaos could ensue if they fell forward and broke their tethers. The English nineteenth-century traveller, Major Dixon Denham, describes the care taken by the cameleers: 'the Arabs hang with all their weight on the animal's tail, by which means they steady him in his descent. Without this precaution, the animal falls forward, and, of course all that he is carrying goes over his head.'[6]

At water holes, the caravan encountered large numbers of camels and goats with their herders – small, taciturn men with impressive moustaches and prominent hook noses, wearing traditional wide-sleeved white smocks and calf-length trousers. With long leather whips slung diagonally across their shoulders and leather amulets and short knives hanging from their upper arms, they were a distinctive, independent breed, who seemed inseparable from their animals.

One of the female slaves had developed a swelling in her thigh and could not walk. Selim led the camel on which she rode for nearly a month while crossing the desert. He records:

> She grew worse and worse every day until she died and was buried in the sand, without coffin or anything, while her death was not commemorated by the shedding of a single tear. Such are the horrors of the slave trade. Well do I remember the evening of her death. The sun was going down, the azure sky appeared to witness the end with calmness and composure, while the surrounding aspect threw deep gloom over all our proceedings. I was thrown far back behind the rest of the travellers; my fellow companion in slavery began to totter in her saddle, and death was soon announced by her falling from the camel. She was a native of Durfur – a woman in the zenith of her life. The death of this unfortunate female put me in permanent possession of the camel during the remainder of the journey.[7]

European travellers on these trading routes often commented on the death toll of men and beasts evidenced by the sheer quantity of bones strewn along the way. Fearsome sandstorms which could bury people alive constituted a major hazard. Massaia gives a graphic description of one such storm:

> As the storm approached nearer and nearer we stopped and unloaded the animals; the men told me to get between the two boxes, wrap myself in the covers, and if the storm were to come over us, to shake myself now and again. Suddenly we were enveloped in intense darkness, and thick sand began to rain down. Placed between the two boxes, I thought only of freeing myself from the sand that fell in great quantity and dropped like water on both sides of me. Shortly afterwards, I began to feel an ever increasing weight on me, despite my efforts to shake it off, and free myself from it. Being wrapped in the covers I was unable to see whence this came, and to tell the truth I was confused, not knowing what to do. At this moment there came into my mind the story I had heard of the thirty Egyptian soldiers who had been buried alive in that very desert. This thought was so frightening that I began to make greater efforts, and so I managed gradually to raise myself and shake off that mass of sand under which I was buried.

The storm passed after about twenty minutes, and Massaia's boxes 'were buried under two spans of sand; of the water bags there was no trace at all!'[8]

Camels were remarkably well adapted to survival in desert conditions, as Fergus Fleming writes in *The Sword and the Cross*:

> Introduced to Africa from Asia in about the first century BC, the camel is a unique example of nature's engineering, adapted like no other beast to desert conditions. Its feet are

> spongy and do not sink into the sand. It stores its energy as fat in its hump, the size of which provides an accurate measure of its vitality. (When pushed to its limits, the hump disappears.) Its stomach holds 200 litres of water and when those are exhausted, it can survive for two or three days on the moisture left in its body tissues, moreover it can lose more than a quarter of its body weight with no ill effect and make it up again in a few minutes. The camel's blood does not thicken in heat, as happens to other animals, so it does not suffer from heatstroke. It can eat almost anything from grass to the leaves that grow on the desert acacias, known as camel-thorns. And it travels at an energy-efficient pace: trotting, it manages maybe six kilometres per hour; when pressed it will go nine; and in emergencies it will move at twenty, but for only a few minutes. Rarely it can be provoked to high speeds: there are tales of camels covering more than 300 kilometres in two days. But, although capable of great endurance, its stamina is unpredictable: it does not flag like normal beasts but keeps up a steady pace until, without warning, it keels over: When it is at the end of its tether, it suddenly stops, cowers down and dies with considerable dignity, and a far-away expression, as if its thoughts are elsewhere. It has a slightly roguish look, as if to play one splendid, final trick on its master.[9]

The rate at which camels could be lost is extraordinary: in 1899 the French army officer François Lamy recorded the loss of 929 camels out of an original 1,004 in one expedition across the Sahara. Giovanni Beltrame, travelling through Nubia in 1861, dedicated several pages of his journal to the remarkable powers of endurance of camels: 'Some of the *hajins*

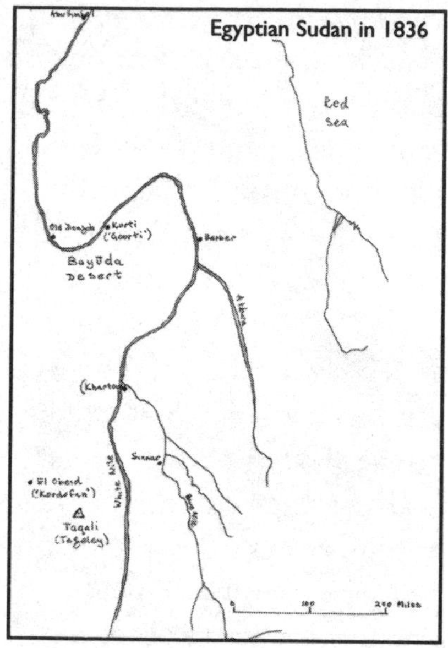

[camels] can continue twenty-four hours without respite. During this time they cover a distance equivalent to five days' ordinary march, and they are also able to average about sixty miles a day for six to seven days running.' Referring specifically to the route that Selim followed between Kordofan and Asyut on the Nile, Beltrame says, 'It is not rare for two or three camels to die under their loads on these long journeys, while others arrive at their destination so exhausted that they are unable to make the return journey.'[10]

Having covered a distance of close on 1,000 miles, Selim's caravan eventually reached Dongola, where the goods were divided between Achmet, Mehemet and Jubalee. Selim was taken by Jubalee as a slave for his wife, and subsequently was sold several times before being acquired by a wealthy Arabian Jew to look after his store in the main market of Dongola. Selim found himself in the largest house in the neighbourhood, superbly furnished with fine carpets and divans. The merchant's wealth came from the many spices and gums gathered from the district, and his family was dressed in rich silks. One day Selim and another slave, Salama, were working in their master's shop when they discovered a pistol and some powder:

> Curiosity induced us to load it. Being the first time I had examined a pistol closely, I desired Salama to fire. He went

> to the window, and putting the mouth of it out to the open air, fired it off, and loaded it again, asking me to fire it off next. Instead of using the same precautions as he did, I fired it off in the shop, which caused a great smell of powder in the arcade. This induced the neighbours to investigate every place closely, who found that the greatest smell proceeded from our shop. They accordingly took hold of Salama, and would have thrashed him had he not put the blame upon me. I now took to my heels and ran for it, but my limbs were not sufficient to escape so many pursuers in the arcade; in consequence I was captured, and received such a thrashing as I did not forget in a very short time. Luckily our master was away from the shop at the time of this occurrence. Contrary to our expectations, he only gave a laugh when he was informed of our conduct.[11]

One day after work, Selim had an astonishing coincidental encounter on the banks of the Nile with his old friend Medina, who took him to her master's house and introduced him to the other young slaves there. Medina and Selim managed to meet on several occasions; she was with her fifth master, he with his seventh. Always they parted sorrowfully, as if for the last time.

It was not long before Selim was sold again, this time to a Berber from Nubia called Hemet Hether. Selim had apparently been strongly recommended to him by Jubalee as an experienced traveller and cameleer. He was taken by his new master to his birthplace at Korti, a month's journey from Dongola, much of it through desert. *En route* they passed the famed temples of Abu Simbel. Selim's claim to being a 'seasoned cameleer' before he was even in his teens might be queried, but to this day these skills are often acquired very young. The modern desert traveller

John Hare records the skill and confidence of a small girl:

> Our travelling companion had with him his daughter, a tiny bare-footed tot of about six or seven, who wore nothing to cover her head and was dressed in a nondescript cotton shift. She was a very solemn little thing, who took her difficult and responsible task immensely seriously. Balanced precariously on one of their camels which was roped to the other four, she successfully negotiated the quintet over countless dunes. Day after day she carried out her arduous task, never complaining, hardly uttering. Her competence with camels was staggering. She bedded them down at night and ensured they were fed and watered with the utmost efficiency.[12]

With Selim were two other slaves, a little Arab-featured girl from Sennar and another boy from Darfur. At Korti, where he stayed for three months awaiting the slave boat to Cairo, Selim was put in charge of the oxen which drove a *sakya,* or water wheel, lifting water from the Nile into the adjacent fields. He gives a good description of the system of irrigation used by the poorer people, the *shadouf:*

> consisting of a long lever suspended between two pillars of wood, a rope with a bucket being attached to one end of it, and a lump of mud or a stone at the other to act as a counterweight. The person who draws the water lets down the bucket four feet below him into the river, and dipping it full of water, raises it, with the aid of the weight at the other end of the lever, some five or six feet high, where it is emptied into a canal, which conveys it to the fields.[13]

Here Selim also saw the tall and elaborate pigeon houses of the Egyptians, palms standing on their pedestals of mud and, in the wake of the ploughing oxen, the darting white cattle egrets. All around were fields of sugar cane, which the *fellahin* chewed raw for its sweet juice. In the villages, people and animals were all mixed up together, with animals sometimes quartered in houses and donkeys, camels and goats wandering at will through the streets, where it was not unusual to see buffalo lumbering by.

Selim also comments on the oppression of the Nubians by the Egyptian government, with press gangs enforcing military service and punitive taxes being levied on water-wheels, palm trees and other local resources. The tyranny amounted to enslavement, and it was not unusual for people to flee into the desert. (Even fifteen years later, the severe oppression of the *fellahin*, exacerbated by the forced labour requirements of the Suez Canal construction, was detailed by Lady Lucie Duff Gordon in her *Letters from Egypt*.) Hemet Hether, Selim's master, gave one of his children, Haroun, the task of teaching Selim the tenets of the Muslim religion. Selim says that Haroun:

> commenced his task by seating me on the ground, tailor fashion, and by holding up one finger before me, saying at the same time '*Allah wahed*' (God is one); but I so incorrigibly persisted in affirming that there were two Gods that my master was compelled to send me to the sheikh for better tuition. The old sheikh very wisely ordered me to look after his sheep and cows, so that I never heard anything more of the mysteries of the Muhammedan faith.[14]

This passage from his memoir is significant in confirming that Selim was not a Muslim, and was therefore at risk of being castrated to serve as a eunuch. Selim had to spend some three months at Korti awaiting the slave boat to Cairo, having in the meantime acquired yet another master, who had recently married a young woman with whom Selim was taken to live:

> In many of the eastern countries, and particularly Egypt, a man is not confined to one wife, but can keep as many as his abilities will allow him. My master's recent marriage was the cause of raising a deal of jealousy on the part of the old one. He chiefly resided at the house he had built for the former, and when the latter met him they were sure to quarrel about something or other. On one occasion, being sent with some corn to the old lady's, on a donkey's back, she would not allow me to empty the sacks, so I had to stand for about half a day to await my master's arrival. On his coming up to me, he asked me why I did not empty the sacks? I told him my reason; after which he went into the house, and a quarrel ensued. The neighbours gathered about the house, and tried to prevent the quarrel; but, my master being in a passion, they found great difficulty in getting him quieted. After he had broken a great number of things, they managed to get him out of the house, and I obtained liberty to empty my sacks and return home. My master also returned to his new wife's, and never went back to Goortie [Korti], till within a few days of leaving for Cairo. The slave ship landed in its season at Goorti, and took us on board.[15]

After his time at Korti, Selim was taken down the Nile by slave ship, spending three months at Dake, and changing boats at the various cataracts after walking overland around these. He records seeing other slaves being punished by flogging for falling sick on this journey. Selim's account gives a brief description of the ancient monuments at Dake, Asswan, Calabashe, Thebes, Luxor and the temple of Kharnak, much of this taken from literature read subsequent to his departure from Egypt. However, at the time of his first journey to Cairo, amid the squalid, overcrowded conditions of a slave boat, he would undoubtedly have been much more concerned with his own fate.

> All about the cataracts the land is scattered over with ancient buildings, the ruins of which are grand even to the present day. The most picturesque spot is the island of Phila, the site of the beautiful temple of Isis, and the most sacred spot in ancient Egyptian mythology. The island is pre-eminently beautiful, being covered over with trees, and other luxuriant vegetation. As the author of *Lands Classical and Sacred* says, 'The trees that grow in Egypt are not numerous. There are a few species of the acacia, the sycamores, and the date and doum palms, but the most characteristic part of Egyptian botany are the aquatic plants found on the edges of the lakes and marshes. Of these the lotus and papyrus are identified with the history of Egyptian arts, literature, and religion. The papyrus grew in Lower Egypt, and was therefore an emblem of that country; while the lotus, which flourishes in the upper countries, was emblematical of Nubia and Ethiopia. The papyrus is remarkable in Egyptian history as having been used as a writing material; many of our manuscripts of the Bible were written on leaves of the papyrus.'[16]

The slaves were landed a few miles from Cairo in order, in Selim's words, to make them look 'as fresh as daisies before entering the city'. From this gathering place, they were made to march in military order, adults in the front ranks, youngsters in the rear, flanked by their masters. At the entrance to the city, all were counted by a man appointed for this purpose – almost certainly for calculation of the slave tax:

> When I entered Cairo on a bright, a glorious Egyptian morning, the sun shining without an envious cloud to mock its brilliancy, bulbuls singing from the fruit-bearing hedges of cactus a song of thanks to the Almighty, who in His great and wonderful care for creation, has numbered and set-apart the very sticks and thorns which constitute her nest, I was marched into it a miserable slave, unable to comprehend all the great moving causes around me, and existing only as the property of Hemet Hether, the Berber slave-dealer. Forty of us were counted as we entered the gates of the city, and the man who kept the tally grumbled at seeing so many masters and so few slaves.[17]

Selim was regularly taken to the slave market, where the grown-up slaves were soon bought, but in his words, 'the small live stock remained for a long time'; in his case, for two months. He was eventually sold to his ninth master, a Monsieur Piozzin, staying only a fortnight with him before being despatched to the house of Piozzin's brother-in-law, Robert Thurburn, in Alexandria. Selim had travelled over 2,000 miles over a period of probably not less than a year. This baptism of fire had toughened up the young boy not only physically, but psychologically. He had been obliged to adapt to very different masters and circumstances, and had developed travelling skills which were to stand him in good stead in his later journeys.

CHAPTER FOUR

'The fate of the author was sealed'

The man-degrading merchandize of man,
And death-devoted wretches were the prey,
Whose crimes had cast their heritage away,
Had forfeited for bondage, stripes and toil,
Their birthright freedom, and paternal soil.

SLAVERY HAS BEEN endemic in North Africa and the Middle East since time immemorial. As distinct from the requirements of the of the plantations in the Americas, relatively few slaves in the Islamic world were used as agricultural labour; much more often they were in domestic service, in the army, or kept as concubines – it was said that there were 12,000 concubines in one Cairo harem alone. Whereas the male to female ratio in the Atlantic trade was two to one, the reverse was usually the case in North Africa; many female slaves were recruited as dancers, musicians and singers.

The Koran states that slaves should be treated as people and not simply as possessions and forbids, for example, the separation of a mother from children below seven years of age. Under Islam there was, largely through the females in their domestic environments, a much higher rate of assimilation of slaves into the community than ever was the case for American or West Indian plantation slaves. In some respects, it was more benign than western slavery in principle, but in practice such exhortations were frequently ignored, despite the fact that enslaving Muslims was frowned upon. However, many Islamic slaves in Selim's time were able to gain their freedom and obtain full civic rights, such as they were. In many cases, personal slaves were treated much better than the wretched *fellahin,* or peasants, who suffered greatly under the reign of Muhammed Ali.[1]

The Koran does not favour castration, and so operations were often performed by Christians, such as Coptic priests in Upper Egypt, or done outside Islamic territories. Eunuchs fetched a high price, largely due to the death rate in the course of castration. They were in demand as guards in Turkish harems and were also employed as clerks, administrators and commercial agents: the tenth-century Caliph of Baghdad was reputed to have had some

7,000 black and 4,000 white eunuchs.[2] Nachtigall reports that at one time hundreds of boys were castrated by a ruler to provide eunuchs.[3] Holroyd refers to the brother of a king of Darfur carrying out 150 emasculations of young boys each year for this purpose, the successful operation enhancing the price of the slave to £5.[4] Given his age, Selim was fortunate not to have fallen victim to this practice. Many eunuchs were appointed to senior positions, and some even became rulers in their own right. Military slaves were recruited specifically and were treated differently from other slaves; while compelled to become Muslim, they often had higher chances of gaining their freedom.

At a conservative estimate, 10,000 slaves per annum were being transported across the Sahara in the early nineteenth century, comprising two-thirds of the values of all caravans in the 1850s, adding up to over a million during that century, with a further 450,000 exported via the Red Sea route. In 1821, a single expedition by the Pasha of Egypt carried off more than 10,000 slaves from only four towns, while double the number of captives would be slaughtered in the process. One caravan from Darfur at the end of the eighteenth century comprised over 5,000 slaves.[5] In Selim's province of Kordofan, it was reckoned that 10,000 –12,000 slaves passed through El Obeid each year.[6] During the nineteenth century, the Egyptian slave market turned increasingly to the abundant source of slaves to be had from the Upper Nile. These congregations of slaves were assembled at El Fasher or other oases from where they were transported to such great markets as Es Siout, 250 miles south of Cairo, which received about 5,000–6,000 slaves annually. From the 1820s onwards, Khartoum became another important slave market.[7]

The death rate *en route* to the markets could be as high as fifty per cent, with up to thirty per cent dying in the first ten days after capture, as the slaves had to walk eight to ten hours a day. Nachtigall puts the survival rate across the Saharan route as low as one in four.[8] When marching across the desert, if water ran out, the slaves would be given the blood of ailing or dead camels to drink. It was said that a single short slaving stay in the central Sudan could set up a merchant for life. A caravan might have – in addition to 5,000 ordinary slaves – eunuchs, deaf mutes, dwarfs, ivory, ostriches and other animals, gold, salt, gum Arabic, tamarind and incense, but the most valuable commodity was slaves, who could be traded for horses (twenty slaves for a good animal), weapons, or as currency for the payment of soldiers' wages or taxes. Nor was the trade confined to Arabs: Holroyd refers to a Frenchman, M Vassière, becoming by 1837 one of the largest slave merchants in the Sudan.[9]

The buying and selling of slaves was closely regulated at markets, and taxes were paid on each slave. The Cairo market, where Selim was taken, was known to be unrivalled in its quantity and variety of slaves, particularly female slaves, who were brought not only from Africa but also from the Far East and the Balkans. Abyssinians were favourites, while blondes commanded a high price. In Selim's time, there would rarely be less than 200 slaves on sale, many of them under the age of fifteen years. For voyeuristic Europeans, this market provided a tourist show. Some actually purchased slaves here, usually through a Muslim intermediary. One European, dressed as a Turk, purchased a slave girl for the Egyptian traveller James Burton for £20, describing how the slave children were physically examined in minute detail and questioned as to their Muslim faith.[10]

Holroyd comments on the impression of light-heartedness among the slaves at the market, which he puts down to relief after the terrors of their arduous journeys, and the prospect of a new life with different owners.[11] Their treatment was likely to be far better than under those who had procured them in the first instance and it has to be said that their lot was more tolerable than that of West African slaves destined for the plantations of the West Indies and the USA. Many domestic slaves and concubines were incorporated into Muslim families and, in a number of cases, rose in the social hierarchy to become personages of some distinction. However, some observers commented on the high mortality among slaves after they had reached their final destination, their low fertility, and high infant death rate.[12] There are records of particularly disproportionate numbers of deaths among slaves during the plague outbreaks in Alexandria. Slaves who spoke Arabic fetched a higher price, but there were loud protests if the proposed buyer was a Christian – many slaves had heard fearsome tales of what they could expect at the hand of the Infidel.

If the Alexandria slave market was not open, slaves would simply be marched round the streets, where anyone was at liberty to stop and examine them prior to making an offer. Prices ranged from £1 to £50, with eunuchs valued at a premium. Holroyd considered the slave trade to be generally unprofitable in the 1830s, as there were too many slaves on offer, reducing prices, while the costs of bringing them to market from distant territories was high. He reckoned that ending the slave trade in Egypt would cost a mere £12,000 per annum.[13] The Pasha's troops often received half their pay in the form of slaves, but were frequently cheated by their officers, who greatly inflated the value of the slaves in calculating the balance of the soldiers' wages. The troops in the garrisons of the Kordofan area, such as at El Obeid, would be ordered into the Nuba Mountains for the annual slave hunt, which usually took place in September or October. There is a record of one such hunt in the 1830s, led by the Governor Kurstapha Bey, capturing some 2,187 people, many of them women and children. The depletion of the male population – most of whom were killed defending their homes and family – meant that there were few recruits to the army.

Two years after Selim's departure from Alexandria, a great slave hunt took place on the orders of the Viceroy of Egypt, Muhammed Ali, who commanded that the province of Kordofan contribute some 5,000 slaves, one of his main targets being the Nubans in their mountain strongholds. Fortunately, we have a detailed record of this by Pallme, who accompanied this expedition.[14] The army of hunters comprised 2,400 infantry, 750 Bedouin horsemen, 200 irregular cavalry, 3,000 dromedary riders and 1,200 native irregulars armed with spears and shields, supported by three large guns, and accompanied by a huge number of transport camels. The location of this hunt may well have been in the Taqali district, which had previously been subject to devastating depredations by slavers.

The first village of 196 souls surrendered without a fight, the sheikh telling Pallme that when the Turkish raids began eighteen years before, in 1820, the population stood at 3,000. Another village of 500 was reduced to only 188: 'Every hut was filled with the bodies of the aged and the young indiscriminately, for those who had not fallen by the sword in battle, had put themselves to death to elude the dreadful fate of captivity.' However, one group of hill tribesmen, armed only with spears, put this formidable army to flight.

The Nubans were being enslaved at the rate of around 10,000 a year and between 1820 and 1835 the area must have lost as many as 150,000 people. Despite the relative success in repelling the invaders in 1838, they had suffered severe losses and Selim would have undoubtedly been caught up in this warfare had he not been captured a few years earlier. In the mid-nineteenth century, the tyrannical Nasir wad Abkr promised to pay a tribute of 5,000 slaves to the Turkish Pasha, in addition to a substantial quantity of ivory, to support his claim to kingship over Taqali.[15] However, in his memoir, Selim castigates the United States, avoiding mention of either British or Islamic involvement in slavery, other than in his own case:

> Thus many of these poor creatures are brought to a level with the brute beasts, by the inhabitants of the federal government, [the United States], who pretend to profess the principles of freedom and Christianity in their truest light. The selling of these captives stimulates others to kidnap some of the poor natives, and carry on a brutal traffic in buying and selling human victims for the gratification of their ambitious propensities. In this manner the fate of the author was sealed.[16]

In 1833, prior to Selim's capture, the British government passed the Abolition of Slavery Act; until that time it was far from uncommon for English gentlemen to purchase slaves in Egypt which was under the suzerainty of the Ottoman Empire. James Burton owned at least three slaves, if his journals are to be believed, all of them women (one Greek). Some even married their slave women and brought them back to Britain. Neil Cooke, who has written about British travellers in the Near East, claims that 'the English appear to have looked upon buying slaves as being part of the lifestyle of an upper-class Turk. Copying, they believed, would help to assimilate them into Egyptian society by maintaining the higher rank associated with ownership.'

Slavery, albeit on a different scale, still exists today in North Africa. In recent years, the Nuba Mountains have been subject to devastating raids from the Arab north, apparently with the support of the Sudanese Government in what some have claimed to be 'ethnic cleansing' or genocide. This has in turn spawned a bloody rebellion of Nuba, allied to the Sudan People's Liberation Army, embracing much of the Christian south. Most of the raids are conducted by the traditional enemies of the Nuba, the Arabic-speaking Baqqara, themselves poor cattle herders. In 1995, more than 300 women and children were taken from a single village in the Nuba Mountains. Some of these raids by militias are supported by the army, closely following the model of the officially sanctioned slave hunts of the nineteenth century, even including the open selling of slaves in the markets by army officers.

One of the most moving testaments to the continued existence of Muslim slavery comes from the Nuba Mountains, where the twelve-year-old Mende Nazer was captured in a village raid in 1998. Her full story is told in *Slave: The True Story of a Girl's Lost Childhood and her Fight for Survival.* Modern slavery in this region involves the slaughter of adult males and the capture of women and children. Boys are frequently sold as cattle herders, while girls and women are put into domestic service or used as sex slaves. The going price for a slave in 2004 was about £100. What is remarkable about Nazer's horrifying narrative is how closely it mirrors Selim's experience, over 160 years earlier. Her description of village life and culture could almost have been that of the young boy in 1834, with rain festivals, shared meals, hunting trips, wrestling matches, and, not least, close and loving family relationships.

CHAPTER FIVE
Robert Thurburn of Alexandria

He knew no friend, nor deem'd a friend was nigh,
Till the sweet tones of Pity touched his ears,
And Mercy bathed his bosom with her tears.

THE FEARFUL YOUNG Selim must have wondered if he had arrived in another world when he came into the Thurburn household in Alexandria, sometime in 1835 or 1836. Almost certainly the first thing to have happened would have been a good soap and water scrubbing from head to toe by the English housekeeper, followed by the issue of clean clothes and a meal, before being shown to his sleeping quarters at the back of the house, which were clean if bare. 'The Sycamores' was an imposing European-style house like others around the Place des Consuls, built by the Viceroy, Muhammed Ali, for the accommodation of the many consulates establishing themselves in this important commercial centre. The fine square of palatial buildings contrasted with the foetid alleys which were the introduction for any traveller making his way from the port to the heart of the city.

Never would Selim have imagined that he would inhabit a house with tall-ceilinged, separate rooms for every function, surrounded by large windows that were screened and shuttered to keep the rooms cool in the heat of the Alexandrian summer. The town garden, occupying six acres, was full of fruit trees and shaded arbours. In the main office, the dusty business ledgers were piled up on a huge desk of English oak, and the adjacent library contained more books than Selim could ever have thought existed. Shown around by the kindly housekeeper, he could only marvel at the solid furniture, brocaded drapes, gilt-framed pictures depicting strange foreign scenes; most frightening of all was a tall mirror in which he saw a small black figure which imitated his movements, like a ghost. And those around him, from the Italian butler to the couple he came to know as Mr and Mrs Larking, spoke amongst themselves in a strange clipped tongue, which bore no resemblance either to his native Taqali or to Arabic, of which he had a rudimentary knowledge. All was strange and overpowering – it even smelt different from anything he had known, making his nostrils twitch.

A centre of Mediterranean civilisation since earliest recorded times, famous as the residence of Cleopatra and for its unique library, Alexandria had fallen into virtual ruin by the beginning of the nineteenth century. It was renowned for its unhealthy climate and as a city of plague, suffering a particularly devastating epidemic of cholera in 1835, when almost half the population died.

The city was revitalised by Muhammed Ali, who made it the most important administrative and commercial centre in Egypt. Its population rose from 13,000 in 1821 to 60,000 in 1838; about one tenth of the city's residents were foreigners, including 3,000 British, mostly intent on taking advantage of the burgeoning commercial opportunities.

The ruler of Egypt, Ali Pasha, was a former Albanian slave. Astute, albeit poorly educated, his ruthlessness was exemplified when, in 1811, he invited 400 Mameluke leaders to his palace in Cairo and had them all massacred. He admired the power and modernity of the British, if not their culture. Ambitious for industrial progress to finance his schemes, he regarded Egypt as his private farm and initiated the growing of cotton, indigo, silk and opium, but this agricultural development was of little benefit to the Egyptian peasants; the profits financed Ali Pasha's military ambitions and grand projects.[1]

He had another source of funding through granting concessions and contracts to European trading consuls, who saw Egypt and the Sudan as a source of imports such as ivory, gold and gum Arabic, and as a potential export market for manufactured goods, machinery, railways, etc. Some had their eye on the unique antiquities of the Nile Valley which had aroused the curiosity and admiration of the public in London and Paris in the early nineteenth century. While the first British consul in Alexandria, Colonel Ernest Misset, was known for his integrity, his successor in 1815, Henry Salt, became notorious for removing priceless Egyptian artefacts and selling them to the British Museum. Most of the important discoveries and the work of transporting them was carried out by his assistant, Giovanni Battista Belzoni.

The British Consul, Robert Thurburn, had been born at Drum in Aberdeenshire on 18 July 1784, the third surviving son of James Thurburn, who died when Robert was nine years old. His eldest brother Alexander, who was to inherit Drum, was then eighteen. When James died, their mother was still, at the age of thirty-eight, comparatively young. Both Robert and John, his elder brother (who built Murtle House near Aberdeen), left home early to seek careers overseas. They were later to build up a successful cotton business in Egypt – their father's linen business may have decided them on this venture. By 1804 Robert and John were living in Valetta in Malta. In June of that year the brothers moved to Alexandria, where Robert took up an appointment as secretary to Major Missett, Consul General in Egypt, and became increasingly involved in the convoluted politics of the country.[2]

In 1807, after the evacuation of Alexandria by British troops, Missett left for Messina in Sicily, leaving Samuel Briggs as Pro-Consul. Robert was to become a partner in business with Briggs (who in 1805 was asked by Admiral Nelson for the whereabouts of the French Fleet). Robert accompanied Missett to Sicily and returned with him to Alexandria in the summer of that year. Following Missett's resignation in June 1814, Robert applied to succeed him as consul, but Henry Salt was appointed. (When

Salt died in 1827, Robert was greatly affected, describing him as 'the only person in Egypt with whom we lived on terms of sincere and cordial friendship'.)[3] In 1813 Robert married Maria Piozzin. He was twenty-nine and she a year younger. She was the eldest child of Charles Piozzin of Lambese in Provence, France, and of Justine Philips, who was of Italian descent. Their six children were all born at Constantinople, where Charles Piozzin was in business. Maria had originally come to Cairo in 1810 with her first husband, Pierre Anthony Pellegrini de Tibaldi, who had died in Cairo in 1812.[4]

The Piozzin family consisted of three daughters and one son. Rosina (b. 1805), married John Wingfield Larking. Caroline (b. 1808), married Charles Joyce, later friend and business partner of Robert. Upon marriage, Robert acquired four stepchildren aged from two to seven. Maria and Robert had ten children of their own, two of whom died in infancy. When Maria died at the age of forty-two in 1827, she had borne fourteen children. Eight of them were left for Robert to bring up. He would have turned for help to his step-daughter-in-law Rosina, then aged twenty-two; Selim mentions her kindness towards him.

At this time, Alexander Thurburn, Robert's nephew, was living in Alexandria. Another nephew, Hugh, brother of Alexander, also lived in the city for a number of years.

In 1833 Robert, by now a partner in the mercantile house of Briggs & Co, was appointed HM Consul at Alexandria. In the same year, he accompanied Lady Franklin, the redoubtable wife of the famous Arctic explorer, on a trip up the Nile. This formidable woman found him agreeable enough, but somewhat serious.[5] The following year, Mark Piozzin (Robert's brother-in-law, who had purchased Selim in Cairo) was appointed Vice-Consul in Cairo.

Robert was active on the committee of the Board of Health of Alexandria. He was interested in the application of scientific principles and proposed a logical approach to the classification of epidemics of cholera and plague. He queried the efficacy of quarantine, being strongly opposed to the shutting up of the inhabitants in their houses during these outbreaks.[6]

On Robert's resignation from his consulship in 1839, he was succeeded by JW Larking, his step-son-in-law, husband of Rosina Piozzin (b. 1805). From at least 1835 Robert had moved into partnership with Charles Joyce in the firm of Joyce Thurburn and Co.[7] Charles was also Robert's step-son-in-law, husband of Caroline Piozzin (b. 1803). The extended family represented a powerful dynasty in Egypt at this time, and were deeply involved in its politics and commerce.[8] Colonel Patrick Campbell, the British Consul General in Cairo, personally commended Robert to Lord Palmerston, the Foreign Secretary, in 1836, in a letter which Robert himself brought back to England. After meeting Palmerston, Robert was presented by him to the young Queen Victoria at her first leveé.[9] It was to Lord Palmerston that Selim was many years later to address his proposal for the 'Amelioration of Africa'.

It is often impossible from the records to distinguish the two brothers, John – the elder – and Robert, both merchants and trading consuls. John was a partner with Robert in the well established British trading house of Briggs, which enthusiastically supported Belzoni's work, although it is not known if either of the Thurburns was directly involved in what today would be widely regarded as the theft of national treasures. However, as assistant consul to Salt, Robert Thurburn would have been well aware of his commercial activities. Briggs after his departure from Alexandria was to become Ali Pasha's sole commercial agent in England and would undoubtedly have had profitable relations with the Thurburns in this capacity.

Although it was not often observed, the distinction between official government appointed consuls and trading consuls was that the former were salaried and therefore not expected to engage in business, while the latter had no such restraints. Robert Thurburn was known to have the ear of the Viceroy and was in a very good position to introduce British travellers and entrepreneurs. A consul might arrange a meeting between a railroad company and a member of the royal household who owned land along the Nile, taking a fee from each, often in the form of stock – the ultimate goal being to persuade the Viceroy to grant a concession.[10] There was fierce competition between the merchant houses.

There are numerous references in travellers' journals to the introductions to the Viceroy effected by Thurburn.[11] John Lewis Burckhardt, an indefatigable North Africa explorer, referred to Thurburn as a man of 'great information'.[12] The geologist and ivory hunter John Petherick, subsequently British Consul at Khartoum, was also grateful to him for his part in gaining a commission from the Viceroy to survey the mineral potential of Kordofan in the Sudan:

> He [Ali] turned to Mr T. a wealthy English [*sic*] Alexandrian merchant, with whom he had for many years been connected in business, who had introduced me, and conversed with him on the state of the market, the stocks of grain, seeds and cotton, displaying a memory of extraordinary capacity and a most intimate knowledge of the state of his commercial and agricultural affairs.[13]

Joyce Thurburn and Co was one of the first European enterprises to obtain ivory from the Upper Nile (the price of ivory doubled between Khartoum and Cairo). Their company agent was Antoine Brun-Rollet, a Sicilian, who was for a time a clerk to Vassière, a notorious French slave trader at Khartoum. It is not known whether the British firm had any connection with the slave trade, but almost certainly slaves would have been used in ivory hunts.[14]

Robert Thurburn gained for himself the lucrative contract to ferry passengers across the desert from Cairo to Suez and would almost certainly have discussed the plan to construct the Suez Canal with its driving force, Ferdinand de Lesseps, French Consul at Alexandria in 1832 and subsequently at Cairo. Samuel Briggs had convinced the Pasha of the trade benefits of this route, stimulated in the 1830s by the development of steamships. With the canals completed in 1869, travellers could avoid the long sea journey round the Cape *en route* to India, and this principle underpinned Selim's later proposal for an east–west overland railway across Africa.

Robert Thurburn was both a founder of the Egyptian Transit Company and a director of the East India Steam Navigation Company, which commenced a monthly steamship service between Suez at the head of the Red Sea and Calcutta, and utilised the shorter journey times being achieved by travel through France and thence to Alexandria.[15] There are many accounts of the danger and discomfort of the two-day journey across very arid desert between Cairo and Suez and there was frequent complaints about the primitive and filthy accommodation, not to mention the hazards of predatory Bedouin. By the mid-nineteenth century, however, some 15,000 passengers were travelling this desert route annually.[16] It is just possible that Selim might have accompanied

Robert Thurburn on it at some time during his stay in Alexandria, but that is speculation.

What is in no doubt is that, after four months in Alexandria, Selim accompanied the Thurburn family (complete with housekeeper and Italian servant Jacquomo) on a month-long tourist trip up the Nile as far as the first cataracts to view the great antiquities.[17] Given Thurburn's wealth and position, they would have travelled in considerable style, with every possible comfort. There could hardly have been a greater contrast to the wretched circumstances in which the young slave had travelled the same route only a short time previously, now properly fed and clothed by the indulgent Thurburns.

In March 1836, Robert left Alexandria for a seven-month extended leave, taking most of his household along with him, including Selim, the Larkings, his housekeeper and her husband. This was Selim's first steamboat journey. In his memoirs he describes being teased *en route* to Malta by the sailors, who assured him that the vessel ran on wheels. The housekeeper and her husband were sent on to England. After quarantine at Lazarett in Malta, the rest of the party sailed on to Messina in Italy – but a violent storm forced them to return to Malta. When they eventually reached Messina, they were met by Robert's nephew, Hugh Thurburn, and stayed at his house.

Leaving the Larkings at Naples, the Thurburns then travelled overland to England and thence to Scotland, which must have been a very exciting experience for Selim, who was then nine or ten years old. On his return to Alexandria, Robert appears to have left Selim with his sister-in-law Elizabeth at Murtle in Aberdeenshire, where she took the little boy under her wing. This tends to confirm that Robert had no particular interest in him as a potential servant. (Robert died in 1860 in his seventy-sixth year, at Lyons, in France.) Elizabeth was Selim's main mentor, and Selim's dedication to her in his published record of his early life is touchingly grateful. It indicates that he was educated not only by the family, but also at the local school under a dedicated master, and that this education, characteristic of the time, had a strong moral underpinning:

> Hitherto, for these ten years, I have experienced your benevolent care and tuition, and have been elevated far abovc many of my poor countrymcn, whosc minds arc lying with the dust. To whom should I ascribe this work, if not to the patroness of my education? To whom should I dedicate these incidents, if not to the guardian of my younger years? Yes, Madam, to you and to you alone, I now acknowledge my gratitude for the many benefits which I enjoy. Although far distant from kindred and relations – although far from the care of an overlooking mother – I have found in you, madam, a truly good substitute for these wants. I have experienced your goodness in sending me to school, and putting me in the hands of one whose whole interest was absorbed in teaching the young idea how to shoot. In whatever circumstances my lot may be cast, I hope your private admonitions will render me impregnable when attacked by the many vices prevalent in the world.[18]

Robert apparently never settled permanently in Britain. In 1853 he and his step-son-in-law John Larking provided a base in Alexandria for the explorer Captain Richard Burton, who was making his preparations for his famous journey in disguise to Mecca, forbidden to infidels. (Shortly after Robert died, Burton referred to 'my venerable friend, the late Robert Thurburn'). Burton seems to have taken up residence in a hut in the garden of 'The Sycamores', at his own request, to try to maintain his disguise as an Arab physician.[19] Larking was apparently one of his few confidants in this escapade, and Burton dedicated the seventh volume of his *Arabian Nights* to him *inter alia*. Writing from Suez in 1853 *en route* to Mecca, Burton lets Dr Norton Shaw, Secretary of the Royal Geographical Society, know that he will receive a bill from Hugh Thurburn. In a further letter to Norton, writing from Cairo in November of that year he asks: 'If you see Larking, pray give him my best salaam and tell him my throat is safe still – what fun we had on board the steamer! [This almost certainly refers to Burton trying out his disguise on fellow officers, who were thoroughly confused.] Did you receive the note I wrote before leaving Alexandria? I gave it to young Thurburn who wanted sadly to hear your African lecture, perhaps he never sent it on.'[20] Burton, in his usual teasing way, signs himself 'Shaykh Abdullah'. It is something of a coincidence that on the other side of the continent, the same Richard Burton, some seven years, later should pick up Selim to be his factotum, both having shared the hospitality of the Thurburns.

One question among many is why Selim was purchased by Robert Thurburn and brought back to Scotland. There is the possibility that this might have been an attempt to save the boy from an outbreak of plague.[21] However, as mentioned above, in the eighteenth and nineteenth centuries it was not uncommon for Europeans to purchase slaves in North Africa. Often they were regarded as an exotic adornment to the grand houses of those who had made their fortunes in the East. But the law prohibiting trade in slaves in British territories had been passed in 1833, and Thurburn's motivation in purchasing Selim may well have been to prevent the boy's becoming a permanent slave, either in a Muslim household or in the Turco-Egyptian army.

Selim's experience up to his presentation at the Cairo slave market would have taught him the value for his own comfort of being obedient and biddable. His obvious intelligence might have prompted Thurburn to consider the experiment of educating him to see what could be made of him. Thurburn could have been entirely altruistic, at least in terms of the mores of the time. Whatever his motives, he completely altered Selim's prospects.

CHAPTER SIX

'The comforts of a civilised and social life'

Here woman reigns; the mother, daughter, wife
Strews with fresh flowers the narrow way of life;
In the clear heaven of her delightful eye
An angel-guard of loves and graces lie.

MURTLE HOUSE, TEN miles west of Aberdeen, commands an enviable south-facing position on a bluff above the River Dee, famed for its salmon fishing. To the west, the house looks to the dark brooding crags of Lochnagar above the royal estate of Balmoral and the magnificent range of the Cairngorm Mountains. The mansion was built in 1823, on the instructions of John Thurburn, in the neo-Greek style then favoured, complete with roof dome and large external columns, by the fashionable architect of the day, Archibald Simpson.[1] Reflecting the wealth and social position of its owner, it had no fewer than ten bedrooms, a morning room, women's room, billiard room and library, beer cellar and three wine cellars. The drawing room contained both piano and harpsichord, while the parlour had a chamber organ.[2]

Approached through an imposing avenue of trees, it was set amid several acres of walled garden, thirteen acres of pasture and forty acres of plantation. The archetypal demesne of the rich gentry of the time, complemented by 500 acres of shooting ground and a rich salmon fishery extending along one mile of the river, Murtle was regarded as one of the finest estates in north-east Scotland. The tenanted farmland was of high quality alluvial soils and was renowned for maturing crops well in advance of other areas in the locality. Over the years, the Thurburns invested heavily in the development and maintenance of Murtle Mill, which provided them with additional income.

The family, known from the Borders and north-east Scotland, had a long history; their distinguished pedigree has been recorded by one of Robert Thurburn's sons, Lieutenant Colonel Felix Augustus Victor Thurburn.[3] The Borders connection is confirmed by the correspondence in 1830 between Mrs Thurburn, writing on behalf of her husband, to Sir Walter Scott, enquiring about the feasibility of acquiring the property at Smailholm near Kelso, that had been Scott's boyhood home. The records of Murtle estate go back to early mediaeval times, when it was church property.[4] However, prior to John Thurburn's reinstatement of the family fortunes, these had been in decline for some time.

John Thurburn was born in Keith, Aberdeenshire, in 1781. He made his fortune through trade in the Middle East and the Mediterranean in the wake of the Napoleonic Wars, and apparently retired back to Scotland at the relatively early age of forty. He had some business interest with the company of Sandison in Sicily, and his will makes reference to an estate at Ringo near Messina. It provides £50 per annum to Robert William D'Arrigo (or Thurburn, as adopted) of Messina, son of Catherine D'Arrigo. (The inference is that this was an illegitimate son.) John Thurburn married Elizabeth Findlater and they had three daughters. One may have died at birth, and Barbara, his youngest daughter, died at the age of thirty-two in 1858. The surviving daughter, Anna, was the heir to the Thurburn estate following the death of Thurburn's wife in 1872, aged seventy-five. John Thurburn died in 1861, aged eighty. At his death he left £64,000; his estate was separately valued at £12,000 in 1880. Together, this would amount to several million pounds sterling today.[5]

There is no known account of Selim's time in Scotland, but we might surmise some of his circumstances and experience. What follows, therefore, is in part a projection of possible scenarios derived from what is known of Murtle House, from census records and from general social and economic histories of this part of Scotland.

In the period when Selim resided at Murtle – twelve years, from 1836 – there were several important events and developments which would have been a matter of discussion in this educated household. As a result of worsening conditions on the land, the pace of emigration was increasing and the local Aberdeen newspapers carried regular advertisements for those willing to take a stake in the New Brunswick and Nova Scotia Land Company. There were important advances in communications, with the introduction of the Penny Post in 1840 and the expansion of the railways, including the construction of the Deeside line, with a new station at Murtle, no doubt promoted by John Thurburn, who had invested heavily in railway stock.

In 1845, the great potato famine in Ireland not only provoked riots in Inverness, where the military used bayonets to disperse crowds protesting against potato prices, but also created a crisis in the cities, with overwhelming numbers of economic refugees coming into Scotland. Overseas the British Empire marched on, annexing New Zealand, Hong Kong and Natal. Scottish soldiers were at the forefront of many campaigns, such as that waged against the Afghans in 1838–42. Scotland, only slowly becoming industrialised and urbanised, was still largely a conservative, rural country. The estate of Murtle, with its traditional hierarchies – from the wealthy and influential landowner, down through the tenantry to the landless farm workers and domestics – mirrored that conservatism exactly.

Even after his introduction to the style of European living in Alexandria, Selim is likely to have been more than impressed by the grandeur of his new home at Murtle and its situation. After the ochre colouring and dust of Egypt, the cool, damp greenness of the Scottish landscape would have been a revelation, as were the icy winds which swept down from the snow-covered Cairngorms from late autumn onwards, when the Dee in flood turned a turbulent tea colour and the great firs bent and creaked in the winter gales. That he was deeply affected by his surroundings is reflected in a poem, 'Scene from the Dining Room Windows of Murtle', which he wrote some years later, in the flowery language typical of the time:

The windows of the dining hall
A beauteous view of west command,
One would not think 'twas nature's earth,
But some romantic fairy land.

The scene beheld still further west
Shows hilly wilds and distant glens –
Romantic, lovely, when compar'd
With Murtle's fertile lowland plains.

In the middle of the same poem he makes reference to a little house adjacent to a field:

This house was built in former days
For one of Afric's antlered tribe.
Its roof is thatched – its peering top
The Turkish banner doth describe.[6]

Here Selim almost certainly refers to a stable for some sort of antelope brought back, no doubt at considerable expense, by John Thurburn, following the fashion of rich collectors of eastern exotica. The poem appears to be something of an afterthought, as it does not appear in either of the published versions of his early life, but is contained as an endpaper in the privately bound copy held by Robert Thurburn's great-great-grandson, Andrew Thurburn.

Selim would have been reminded of his origins by the large map of Egypt hanging in the billiard room, while in the library he was at liberty to pore through the many volumes on the history, geography and antiquities of the Middle East and Africa. It is not known how long Robert stayed at Murtle House following his arrival in 1836, before he returned to Alexandria and his family in late 1837, leaving Selim in Scotland. John Thurburn's obituary in the local press suggests that he himself was at Murtle for much of his life, taking an active part in public affairs over forty years.[7] However, Selim's fulsome dedication to her in his description of his early life suggests that John's wife, Elizabeth Thurburn, was mainly responsible for his welfare:

> I return my grateful and sincere thanks to you for the great interest you have taken in my education, by which means I have been brought from African darkness to a knowledge of the comforts of a civilised and social life.[8]

In Scotland, Selim witnessed not only the quality of life that the wealthy and influential enjoyed, but also saw for himself the conditions of the rural poor, which in some respects compared unfavourably with those of his native village. Selim had come into a highly structured and hierarchical world, with the big house of Murtle at the hub of a series of circles of influence in a rural – but not isolated – parish, in a region with its own distinctive identity and culture. At the centre of that hub was the heritor or laird, who took pride in his paternal oversight of an extended 'family' of servants, tenants and labourers, all dependent on his patronage and prosperity.

The agricultural revolution of the previous century had transformed much of the landscape, from the improvement of

Plan of Murtle estate in the mid-nineteenth century

the stony moorland for stock grazing with the new breeds of Aberdeen Angus beef cattle and the crossbred sheep, to the now fertilised and enclosed croplands. This had not been achieved without backbreaking work, both of boulder removal and the excavation of new drains lined with stones; even hand-digging of the soil had to be resorted to, where the plough could not go. The horse was still king, gradually taking over from oxen for ploughing with the more common lighter ploughs, while the new reapers and winnowers were replacing the wearisome flail and hand-cutting of oats and barley.[9] With longer leases, tenants were given an incentive to improve their farms by enclosure and application of guano and crushed bones, while the lairds took on the responsibility of planting up hedgerows and woodlands for both amenity and sport. Everywhere, the old primitive animal sheds were being torn down to make way for more modern stables and byres, now separated from living quarters, usually round a square steading.[10]

According to Burton, after Selim's departure from Scotland, he pined for a cottage there, and 'would have accounted himself passing rich on £40 a year'. This sum would be wealth indeed for the average male farm servant, whose income, albeit supplemented by 'payment in kind' of oats, barley, potatoes and peas, would be considerably less than half that amount. If such a servant was married and his wife was able to spin, their joint incomes might be £28 a year.[11] Farms were increasing in size and a good-sized one would have a grieve, or overseer, a foreman ploughman and an ordinary ploughman for each pair of horses, a cattleman and a shepherd – all hired at the half-yearly feeing fairs.[12] A married shepherd would most likely have had his own small, heather-thatched cottage where the owner also allowed him ground to keep a cow, a potato patch and kailyard. In addition, he would be provided with six bolls of meal, although he had to cut his own peats from the moss. He would be full of praise for the new crossbred sheep, which combined the toughness of the skinny hill Blackface with the heavier build of the Cheviots.

Selim would have seen that the community was dependent on specialist skills and trades, from the blacksmith to the carpenter, the harness and saddlemaker to the itinerant tailor. In the Sudan, families ground their own meal, but in Scotland it was more usual for farmers to bring their corn to a central mill, often rented by an owner, allowing the miller to charge his own price – a source of considerable resentment. The outstanding difference was the opportunity for education in Scotland, even if the demands of work on the farm often frustrated its uptake, especially where high rents required the whole family to contribute their labour, to the exclusion of all other activity, including schooling.[13] Around a big estate such a Murtle, there was much casual employment for the cottagers, particularly women and children: picking stones, pulling turnips, and weeding paths or raking leaves in the woods and gardens. Some of the cottagers had handlooms which helped to supplement their income; weavers were an important source of agricultural labour at harvest time.

If Selim accompanied John Thurburn on estate inspections, he would have gained an understanding of the life and conditions of the tenantry. He certainly must have made comparisons with the conditions for farmers in his homeland. Many of those on the land in north-east Scotland were peasant farmers, largely subsisting on their own production. What they had in common with the Taqali villagers was a strong sense of the value of land and their part in the community, while priding themselves on their self-reliance. Typically they were sober, frugal and industrious, always on the lookout for those small savings and hard-won improvements which might enable them to enlarge their acreage and increase their yields. But Selim would soon have learned that not everyone enjoyed 'the comforts of a civilised and social life'.

The habitations of the gangs of unmarried farm workers were poorer than many in the Sudan, being a thatched shed, or bothy, without a ceiling, with a single door and an earthen floor. The room would be unpartitioned, with double beds (the mattresses filled with chaff) for six men along the walls and an open fire at one end. Usually in such quarters the only furniture consisted of the two 'kists' or wooden chests allotted to each man for his meal and clothes, which took up much of the floor space; these also served as chairs. Each man was given three pints of unskimmed milk daily (in a week six men would consume the milk of two cows) and twenty pounds of oatmeal per week, and they catered for themselves.[14]

Even under these primitive conditions, there was a strict hierarchy, with the senior ploughman taking precedence, even to the extent of sleeping with the next in line, the assistant ploughman. If one of the young farm labourers, in a rash moment of martial enthusiasm, took the Queen's shilling at a feeing fair in Aberdeen and went off to join the Gordon Highlanders, each man would move up a notch. Everyone took their turn bringing in the peats provided by the farmer, cleaning, carrying in water (since there was none in the bothy) and making the morning porridge in the large three-legged iron pot which served for all cooking.

The ploughmen definitely considered themselves a cut above the rest, and took great pride in their fine Clydesdale horses, which were groomed with the greatest care: when they were to be taken into town, their harnesses were blackened and polished till they shone.[15] These men had a subtle skill with the animals and were devoted to them. They were up before 5 o'clock in the morning to feed and water their charges, returning at 7:30 for breakfast, having spent the intervening hours threshing, as they did also in the evening when winter darkness forced the men inside. We can imagine that many of Selim's schoolmates cherished the ambition to be a ploughman with their own pair, and playground games no doubt reflected this, to the extent of roping in a couple of other school friends to act as horses, with a length of binder twine as reins.

Farm workers were expected to keep working even in bitter snow or rain. Their monotonous diet of meal, potatoes and milk only varied if they found some hen eggs the farmer's wife had missed. Everyone was up before dawn and retired early; with a guttering tallow candle and only the light from a low-glowing peat fire, there was little incentive to read, even if the men had the capacity. Later Selim might have wondered whether this was not simply another form of slavery, not dissimilar to what he had escaped from, albeit the farm workers had the option, which they not infrequently took, of ending their six-month contract with an employer and seeking a better position at the feeing markets.

Selim would have been even more familiar with the household servants and their work, from John Taylor, the dignified general overseer of the proprietor's house, to the butler, George MacLennan, whose meticulous standards the boy might well have striven to emulate; it is reasonable to surmise that Selim would learn much from MacLennan that would later impress Burton.[16] Although domestic work was endless and poorly paid – female servants in the 1830s were lucky to get £3 half yearly – these situations were much sought after, particularly by young women, whose wages made a valuable contribution to their family's income.[17] Just as important, they had security from real want. They were usually well fed and comfortably, if not luxuriously, housed in the servants' quarters. It was reckoned that the total cost of maintaining a male servant at this time was about £40 a year, and £12 for a woman.[18] Some, such as the coachman, had their own quarters adjacent to the stables.

It was rare to find a female servant much over the age of forty, since most were married by this time.[19] As they were usually put to work at an early age, their education was often neglected, and those from more remote areas required careful training and supervision for some time before they could be relied on. After their experience of the lifestyle of the big house, some of these women, especially if married to one of the richer farmers, introduced some of its refinements into their own home, while others disdained the proposals of mere ploughmen.

Apart from the male staff, Murtle had a resident cadre of six female servants: cook, kitchen maid, laundry maid, dairy maid, and two house maids[20]: it is likely that they would be up before dawn on the cold, dark winter mornings, cleaning out and lighting the open fires which served the whole house, and in the evenings, carrying the heavy buckets of hot water from the kitchen to provide baths upstairs. The servants were privileged in comparison with most countryfolk, in having meat and fish as part of their diet. Amongst the poorer cottagers, even oatmeal became short before harvest time and the fare was potatoes and more potatoes, consumed in enormous quantities, although Deeside remained unaffected by the grain riots of 1846 and 1848 which swept along the Buchan coast to the north.[21] While the kitchen garden, with its kail, potatoes and peas provided the staff's staple fare, occasionally they had their share of the salmon, leftover rabbit and hare which the gamekeeper brought in: it was he who probably gave Selim his first lessons in shooting, initially with a shotgun and then with a small-bore rifle, a skill which proved valuable in his later expeditions with Burton.

CHAPTER SEVEN

'They hail thee as the stranger's home'

No more the negro dreads the white man's eye;
No more, from hatred to the teacher, spurns
Instruction: gladly he receives the boon
Of science and of art.

ALTHOUGH VISITORS AND special occasions placed extra demands on the staff, there would be a certain excitement among the servants at the prospect of seeing 'the gentry' and distinguished guests, sometimes from foreign parts, and in being issued with the best serving clothes for elaborate dinners, which sometimes required additional help from outside the house, usually involving the wives of tenants. The butler would come into his own on these occasions, issuing instructions to all and sundry, not excluding Selim, one of whose tasks, in a footman's braided blue uniform might be to run out on wet nights with a large umbrella to open the carriage doors of arriving guests and usher them ceremoniously under the shelter of the Grecian portico of Murtle House, before helping to remove their heavy cloaks.

We know from census records that one guest was the venerable John Forbes, a Professor of Oriental Languages.[1] We can also surmise that Forbes would do the honours in opening and ending the meal with a long and heartfelt Scottish grace, delivered in the powerful dialect of his Buchan district. Although Selim knew, from his experience of the parties given by Robert Thurburn in Alexandria, something of the style of European hospitality, he would have marvelled at the sumptuousness of the fare provided for important visitors: at least two soups, followed by fish and various entrées of meat, mutton and game, accompanied by a variety of good French wines from John Thurburn's renowned cellar and ending with spun sugar concoctions and imported fruits for dessert.[2]

When the ladies temporarily retired, the menfolk would light their cheroots as a prelude to a lively discussion on everything from the problems of the potato famine to the rising Chartist movement in Aberdeen and Parliamentary reforms for the poor, in which John Thurburn took a particular interest. It was said of him that he was 'a liberal supporter of every public undertaking'.[3]

On these occasions, the servants would not themselves be able to retire until the cook was satisfied that everything had been scrupulously cleaned and put in its proper place, which meant not far short of midnight. One of these events was likely to be the grand dinner given on 24 April 1849 in honour of Anna Thurburn's wedding the following day in Peterculter to William Osborne Maclaine, a prominent landowner in Kyneton, Gloucestershire. Anna, then aged twenty-five, was the eldest daughter of the Thurburns, who also had another daughter, Barbara, who was the same age as Selim. The wedding celebration would have been attended by a degree of formality, with printed invitation cards being sent not only to friends and relatives, but also to the major landowners and public figures of the district and beyond.

Full use might have been made of Selim (now in his early twenties) and his considerable skills in the elaborate preparations for a party, the like of which the grand house of Murtle had not seen since the wedding of Isabella Thurburn from Nova Scotia in 1836.[4] Everyone would put on their best finery, but no one would be more resplendent than Captain Henry Thurburn, in his gold-braided uniform of the 42nd Madras Native Infantry – the youngest son of Robert Thurburn, home on leave from the East India Company.[5] Anna had made her own claim to fame some seven months earlier, presenting a bouquet to Queen Victoria when she stopped at Murtle *en route* to Balmoral for her first visit – no doubt a major talking point in the district.[6]

The following evening would have been the servants' celebration, with the large dining room cleared for the dance. All John Thurburn's workers and cottagers and their wives and children would be invited. He is likely to have provided a plentiful supply of Deeside whisky as well as home-brewed heather ale – though the butler was charged with the task of ensuring that no one got to a point of inebriation. For some, it is likely to have been the first time they had entered the 'muckle hoose' and they would have marvelled at everything, from the expensive paper on the walls to the fine pictures and gleaming furniture, as they shyly took their glasses of punch. We can see Selim recalling equivalent celebrations in Taqali, when there would have been noisy greetings, and being surprised at the sobriety of this company. However, when the musicians made their appearance and the first of the dances started up, native exuberance is likely to have come to the fore. To the rhythm of pipes and fiddle, we can imagine the company dancing merrily to the old strathspeys and reels made popular by the music and teaching of the Gows from Upper Deeside.

An there was a waddin'! Sic vivers an' drinks,
Sic fiddlin' an pipin', sic dancin' an' jinks;
The haggis e'en hotched tae the piper its lane.[7]

It is possible that they followed the old north-east custom of starting the dance with the *shaimit* reel performed by the bride, her bridesmaids, the bridegroom and his best men, with the bride choosing the music and the male dancers paying the musician his fee. What might have intrigued Selim, after his experience of the class divisions of British society, was the tradition in the north-east of the proprietor and his family joining enthusiastically in the festivities. After the first hesitations, no one would seem embarrassed by this socialising between widely different classes, even if the guests from the south, excusing themselves by their unfamiliarity with the hearty dances, held back. Elizabeth, some twenty years younger than her husband, would have looked regal as she courteously accepted the first quadrille with the grieve, John Taylor, his privilege as the general overseer of the estate.[8]

The reference to 'sending me to school' in Selim's dedication to Mrs Thurburn shows that, although Selim might have received some tuition at Murtle, he attended the local school. Burton specifies that Selim obtained his education 'chiefly at a Scotch school near Murtho, Aberdeenshire'.[9] In his pamphlet of 1853, Selim states that he 'was sent to school' by John Thurburn. The nearest schools were Craigton or Countesswells, but there are no records of these establishments prior to the Scottish Education Act of 1872.

Before schools became the responsibility of the state, they were largely administered and controlled by the church authorities, and the master of a single teacher school in a rural parish was likely to be the local church minister, or 'dominie', as he was referred to in Scotland. Even as early as 1800, the leading landowners in each parish, by law, provided a schoolhouse and funds for the salary of a master, a system which marked Scotland out historically as a leader in democratic public education, with a proud tradition as the most literate country in Europe.[10] John Thurburn would probably have been such a patron, and as such he would have attended any important meetings concerned with the appointment of the teacher and the school's operation, and he would have kept a close eye on his protégé's progress.[11]

In the poorer rural parishes the conditions of the schoolroom could be primitive in the extreme; heating might consist of a meagre fire and barefooted children would be sent home if there was a prospect of snow. The unplaned floorboards were only occasionally cleaned, and the pupils sat in pairs on narrow deal benches. The schoolroom conditions of the time are well illustrated by Thomas Faed in his *Visit of the Patron and Patroness to the Village School* and in Sir George Harvey's *Schule Skailin*. These paintings show how in the smaller country schools it was normal for a single teacher to teach all grades and ages.

A description of such a parochial school in Aberdeenshire in the 1830s states that the instruction given consisted of English reading, writing, arithmetic and Latin, and the salary of the aged master was a mere £26 per annum, to which might be added up to £10 in school fees. It is not surprising that the grossly underpaid dominie would seek every opportunity for supplementary employment. This record also refers to the successful establishment of a parochial library, with a select number of books of history, voyages and travels. More advanced schools would add theoretical and practical mathematics, geography, elementary physics, Greek, and occasionally French or German.[12]

There was still a strong emphasis on the classics, with some science, but virtually nothing on Scottish history and culture. The schoolroom ethos was one of competition, with pupils being promoted or relegated according to their proficiency in reading or spelling tests, and with special attention being paid to copperplate writing. Physical punishment by means of the tawse, or leather belt, for blotted copybooks or inattention was the norm. In some Aberdeenshire schools, there was a large flat stone just outside the door to which pupils who had been chastised could rush at playtimes and take some of the heat out of their wounds, thus earning for it the name of 'the cooling stane'.[13] After his floggings and beatings as a slave, Selim, if he ever was subject to such beltings, might have regarded this punishment as mild. However, given the status of his patron, the teacher would have thought twice before subjecting Selim to undue punishment.

All the scholars were carefully instructed in the principles of the Christian religion and Selim's writing indicates that he became a Christian.[14] In Burton's words, 'he became strongly affected towards Presbyterianism'.[15] The Bible was the foundation of all education in Scotland.[16] Selim would most likely have attended Sunday services and daily worship at Murtle with other members of the household. During his time there, the church in Scotland was in a ferment, with deep schisms occasioned by the practice of landlord patronage and control of church appointments. Such practices were sanctioned by the established Church of Scotland but were vehemently opposed by others, culminating in the Disruption of 1843. The minister and congregation of the church of Peterculter near Murtle was the first in Scotland to build a Free Church in the district.

As heritor, John Thurburn, at least before the Disruption of 1843, would have had a voice in the appointment of the minister, and a dedicated family pew or 'loft' in church, above the congregation. The custom was for the minister to observe the courtesies by bowing to the laird on entry, while the congregation waited for his family's departure before rising to leave – again, the minister's nod was the signal. Sunday was a day of strict Sabbath observance; no visitors would be expected at Murtle and anything other than religious reading might be frowned upon. It did, however, provide the countryfolk with an opportunity to display their 'Sunday best' and, given their primitive living conditions, a visitor might have been surprised how well turned out the farmworkers and ploughmen were in contrast to their workday Irish linen shirts and thick corduroy trousers tied below the knee.

If John Thurburn, undoubtedly the leading landowner, was

typical of others in the area, he is most likely to have opposed the Disruption, which reduced the authority of the lairds in public affairs. There would have been intense discussion of the topic at Murtle, as there was in virtually every household in Scotland, such was the feeling aroused by the most important ecclesiastic event in the nineteenth century. It may well have affected the appointment of the dominie at the school which Selim attended, since this was in the gift of local landowners; in some places this issue caused the most heated divisions between the latter and other authorities. Neither the minister nor the dominie, given the influence of the heritor in their appointments, was likely to have disagreed with the laird in any public matters, while the kirk session, which distributed poor relief in the parish, would be disinclined to give this to someone who dissented from the laird's views. However John Thurburn might not have been one of those proprietors who insisted on his workers remaining with the established church on pain of dismissal, as was not uncommon in the district. We can imagine how bemused Selim was by the passions which this religious dissent created.

Although in the census of 1841 Selim is designated as a manservant, and may indeed have carried out some household duties, it is quite likely that this label was a matter of convenience. He was not in the usual sense a member of the family, a visitor, or an employee, the only categories available on the return. Selim became patriotic to the point of being jingoistic, as can be seen from his 'Ode to Britain':

Britain, thou land of peace and joy,
How strong thy bulwarks are;
Thou standest far above the world,
And that without a par.

Britannia – 'Where e'er I go, the captive I will save'

The 'Ode' also has a certain resonance with his own situation, aptly reflected in the illustration of Britannia surrounded by freed slaves, when he says:

> They hail thee as the stranger's home,
> The freedom of the slave,
> Thy motto is 'Where'er I go,
> The captive I will save.'[17]

In another poem, he lauds the victory of British arms at the battle of Gwalior in India, glorifying Britain's military might, which was of course very much in keeping with the mood of the time. There is no indication of his age when these verses were written, although he may have been in his late teens, given that, when he left Murtle when he was in his early twenties, he would have known that such sentiments would have pleased his patrons.

It appears that towards the end of his time with the Thurburns Selim accompanied John Thurburn on extensive travels. In his 1853 pamphlet, Selim states that under the auspices of John Thurburn, 'I received a liberal English education, travelled with him through many parts of the world, and at last, wishing to establish commercial intercourse between Great Britain and my native country... in 1849, and came up to London'.[18] Burton states that Selim travelled widely in Europe, Asia, Africa, and South America and returned to Africa in 1860,[19] but this date contradicts the evidence that Selim was with Baikie's second expedition up the Niger in 1857. There is no evidence that Selim attempted to make contact with his parental family.

Selim's own statement suggests that his travels with John Thurburn were not confined to Europe, but whether these were for business or leisure purposes is not known, nor in what capacity. He may have accompanied Thurburn as a personal valet, which, together with his experience at Murtle, would have given him a number of skills, quite apart from broadening his education and his first-hand knowledge of the world. By the time he left Murtle for London – there is no indication of why he left – he would have been a fairly sophisticated young man, with an excellent command of English and some awareness of how to comport himself in the society of the time.

CHAPTER EIGHT

'A key to the civilisation of the whole world'

In realms remote, where antient Niger flows,
'Mid woods still locked in nature's deep repose;
Where none has furled the sail – the ventr'ous oar
Has near resounded from the sylvan shore.

ALTHOUGH HIS TRAVELS would have included London (even if only in transit), actually residing in the city would have come as something of a culture shock to Selim. When he arrived there in 1849, this would have been the first time that he was not under the protective wing of the Thurburns, to whose ways he would have become entirely accustomed – he had left behind the peaceful rural existence and greenness of the Deeside country. His address was virtually in the centre of the city that was the hub of a rapidly expanding British Empire – the capital of the acknowledged leader of nations.

By mid century, London's population, at about two and a half million, had doubled in fifty years. It was estimated that some 300,000 immigrants arrived in 1849 alone, not least as a result of the pogroms against the Jews in 1848 and 1850 in Central and Eastern Europe. In 1848, the year before Selim first came to the metropolis,[1] the devastating Irish famine had led to a massive influx, contributing to an excess of labour with consequent low wages and gross overcrowding in the capital. Many of the Irish were employed on construction projects such as the inner London railway system and the London Docks which was then one of the great sights of the city.[2] There was even, in 1851, a proposed submarine railway between England and France.

In 1849 the metropolitan area had suffered some 6,500 deaths from cholera and the sanitary conditions were appalling; many poorer districts relied on stand-pipes in the streets for water.[3] Food was sold from open barrows and carts, in the most unhygienic conditions. Unregulated public burial grounds, full to capacity, with corpses often buried near the surface, led to the contamination of ground waters and the spread of disease.[4] In the year before Selim's arrival, the Public Health Act initiated the construction of a modern and comprehensive sewage system, involving the wholesale digging up of streets for pipe-laying, providing its own quota of noise and dust to the already infernal clamour and dirt. The dirt came not only from the rubbish deposited in the streets and narrow alleyways, but also from the ubiquitous coal fires which blackened buildings and whose soot fouled everything, including the lungs of the residents.

The transport system was chaotic, despite the establishment of the first London railway in 1838 and the laying down of the main railway arteries by the late 1840s. The principal streets were still jam-packed with a slow-moving mass of horse-drawn traffic – the private carriages and broughams of the gentry, stage coaches arriving and departing from the suburbs and beyond, and above all, the hansom cabs – the taxis of their day, conducted by yelling, foul-mouthed coachmen, all competing for fares in an overcrowded market, racing to catch the next fare before their neighbours.[5] Add to this the excruciating noise of the iron rims of speeding wheels on cobbled streets, the cracking of whips and the smell from the plentiful horse dung, and it is easy to see why many Londoners opted for the relative calm of water transport, which plied the Thames between the main stations. The boats were only seriously undermined by the developing railway system of the late 1850s, which also displaced poorer city dwellers from their homes.[6] Many of the wealthy opted to leave their fine houses in central London and move either to the new suburbs, from where they could commute if necessary, or to the country proper, resulting in depopulation and downgrading of the previously fashionable districts of the centre.[7] Selim must have wondered why he had exchanged a rural idyll in northern Scotland for the hell of one of the most overcrowded and noisy cities of Victorian Britain; and with his Presbyterian background, he may well have been shocked by the fact that many London shops were open for trade on a Sunday in order to cater for the many workers who had no other free time to obtain the necessaries of life.

Preparations were well in hand for what was to become the greatest show on earth: the Great International Exhibition of 1851 at the Crystal Palace, the largest glass structure in the world, covering some twenty-one acres. Its central avenue was no less than 1,848 feet in length, incorporating some existing large park trees.[8] The *Illustrated London Evening News* devoted considerable space to its unique system of construction – and to the diversity of the spectators who came from all over to view a wonder of the Victorian world.[9] It certainly made its own contribution to the overcrowding and pressures on the public services of the metropolis, and hardly surprisingly, its high prices. Not only were visitors treated to displays of the latest modern industrial inventions, but it included artefacts and depictions of ancient Egypt, which may have had an effect on other comparable city attractions, including the 'Panorama of the Nile' described below – certainly, promoters of these claimed that their businesses were being damaged.

Selim's ostensible purpose in coming to London was to promote trade between Britain and 'his country' – the latter more likely referring to what was then described as Central Africa rather than simply part of the Sudan – 'with the view to putting an end to the Slave Trade'. One could hardly accuse him of lack of ambition, but in fact this notion had been around for some time. With the almost overweening confidence of the Victorians, he claimed, 'Nothing is impossible in the 19th Century.' The slave trade had been a contentious moral, political and economic issue in Britain for a century, the main focus being the trade from West Africa to the Americas. Attempts at abolition through legislation, embargoes and sea blockades had been only partially successful; slavery was integral to the culture and local economies of much of Africa, while being the mainstay of plantation agriculture in the West Indies and the USA. In Africa, slaves represented both wealth and power; slaves were sold by tribal chiefs for guns and ammunition, which in turn enabled them to carry out raids more effectively.

The anti-slavery movement in Britain had been gathering powerful adherents since the mid-eighteenth century. In 1840, the philanthropist Thomas Fowell Buxton, successor to the great campaigner William Wilberforce, addressed a huge meeting in Exeter Hall in the Strand, organised by the Society for the Extinction of the Slave Trade and for the Civilisation of Africa, and graced by no less a presence than the Prince Consort. It was also attended by David Livingstone, then still a trainee missionary, who was profoundly affected by the occasion.[10] The main thrust of Buxton's case was that slavery in Africa (if not in the Americas) could only be ended by economic displacement, with Africans able to trade homegrown goods profitably, enabling them to purchase the manufactured products of Europe (the textiles and metalware of industrial Britain in particular). Slaves would no longer be a form of currency. This ideology, which Livingstone was later to convert into a popular national cause, was encapsulated in the three Cs: 'Commerce, Christianity and Civilisation'. Its effectiveness lay in its appeal to different interests. The church embraced its moral purpose, traders and manufacturers saw its commercial opportunities, explorers found in it a justification for investigating potential trade routes into the continent, and government saw strategic benefits without direct involvement.

There was one major problem. Apart from access to the coast, Africa was without any modern system of rapid communications to and from its potential markets in the interior. By mid century, Britain had played a major part in developing steam power, then used it to expand its railway system and to greatly reduce the time of ocean voyages. In India and elsewhere in the expanding British Empire, railways were being constructed primarily for military purposes to move large numbers of troops and their equipment to potential trouble spots, for example along the Nile. The first serious attempt to penetrate the interior from the Indian Ocean to the north end of Lake Nyassa by road was started in 1878 under the sponsorship of Fowell Buxton and the Scots shipping magnate William Mackinnon, but it barely covered seventy miles before it was abandoned. It was not until the 1970s that a railway was completed across Tanzania following this proposed route.

Only in the early 1880s would work start to link Lake Nyassa and Lake Tanganyika, providing a trade route via the Zambezi, the so-called Stevenson Road, named for its main financier, James Stevenson of Glasgow.[11] Such was the faith in steam power and its potential that the first steamboats were carried in sections overland to Lake Nyassa in 1862. With the exception of the primarily military railways, all of these time-consuming and expensive projects were aimed at stimulating agricultural production and local trade, with the longer-term objective of removing the incentive for the continuance of the commerce in human beings; in many cases, ivory was the most profitable item until it ran out.

This is the background to Selim's very ambitious and wildly utopian plan, which he hoped to present to Lord Palmerston, the imperious Foreign Secretary, in 1849. In essence it was quite simple: build a railway from east to west across the waist-belt

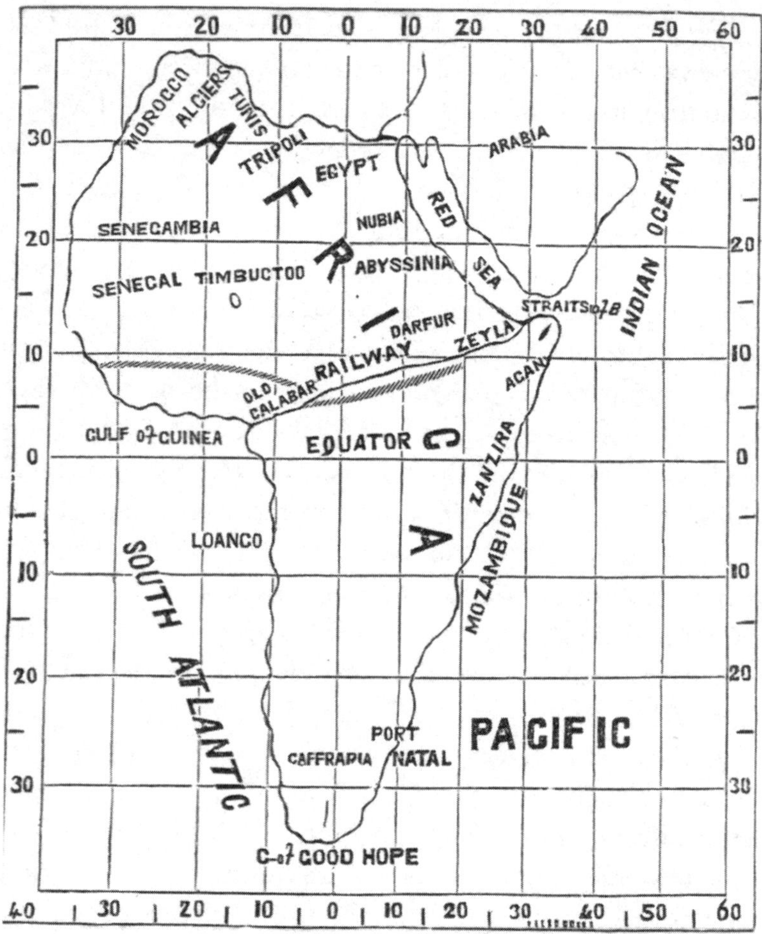

Map showing the route of Selim's proposed trans-Africa railway (British Library)

of Africa, from Zeyla on the Red Sea to Old Calabar on the west coast. Selim prefaced his plan with a summary of his early experiences as a slave and his salvation at the hands of the Thurburns. Palmerston had met Robert Thurburn in 1836, introduced through a letter of commendation from Colonel Patrick Campbell, British Consul General in Cairo, and they had also met at the young Queen Victoria's first leveé. Perhaps this encouraged Selim to believe he might have Palmerston's ear. His *Plan* is prefaced with a panegyric to the humanity of all Britons:

> I have shed tears of joy and gratification while thinking of the kindness of the inhabitants of the United Kingdom towards my countrymen. No person can say to those Africans who have conducted themselves with propriety have not been cordially received by every Englishman, Irishman, or Scotchman. In the British dominions the same protection is held out to every individual, no matter about his colour or clime; and the African, despised and degraded in other countries, is looked upon by every British subject as 'a man and a brother'.[12]

Whether Selim actually believed this, or whether he is being somewhat sycophantic, is open to question. After many difficulties putting forward his plans to the government, he wrote to HM Secretary of State for Foreign Affairs and within a fortnight, was given an audience with a Mr Addington, one of the secretaries in that office, to whom he was able to make his proposals – a remarkable achievement. It is difficult to believe that this was not without some influence being brought to bear by the Thurburns and their friends. However, in May 1853 he was still waiting an affirmative response from government, which, in his words, may have been due to the government 'being in a state of disquietude' at the time. Arising from the *coup d'état* of Louis Napoleon, Palmerston had been dismissed as Foreign Secretary in 1851 for interfering in the internal affairs of France. There was also great trouble in Ireland, with the establishment of the Irish Tenant League in 1850. In that year, without consultation, Palmerston had ordered the British fleet to Greece to support the claim of a British subject to compensation from the Greek government – the beginning of so-called 'gunboat diplomacy.' All in all, it was probably not a good time for a former slave in his early twenties to propose to a reluctant government what must have seemed a harebrained and very expensive scheme to save Africa from itself, notwithstanding Palmerston's passionate anti-slavery speeches.

Selim's high-flown plans were one thing, but meantime he still had to support himself. Amongst educated London society, interest in ancient Egypt was running strong, stimulated by the removal to England of some of the great monumental treasures of that country. These were now on public view in such institutions as the British Museum. There was a craze for all things Egyptian, including incorporation of Nilotic symbols in architecture, most of it in quite inappropriate settings.

Several 'Egyptian Halls' had opened in the metropolis, one of the most famous being in Piccadilly. Founded in 1810 by William Bullock, primarily as a natural history museum, it became the most fashionable place for amusement in London. It was here that Giovanni Belzoni, Henry Salt's accomplice, exhibited his purloined Egyptian antiquities and drawings in 1879. Modelled on an Egyptian temple,[13] the hall could mount several exhibitions simultaneously, ranging from the seriously educational, to what could only be described as freak shows. Also in Selim's favour was the development of 'panoramas', patented by an Edinburgh painter, Robert Barker, following a presentation of this form of entertainment in 1787 in Leicester Square. Initially these were simply illustrated tableaux, often of considerable size, painted on a variety of materials, shown for the education and entertainment of a public which had limited opportunity to see first-hand the exotic scenes depicted.

Just prior to Selim's arrival, moving panoramas had become the rage. A Dundee man, William Hamilton, introduced one of the first dioramas – on the same principle as the panorama – and his *Round the World in 120 Minutes*, was shown around Britain and the continent for eighty years, between 1848 and 1928. One, exhibited between 1848 and 1850, showing the landscapes and features of the Mississippi, was three miles long (though it was probably less than a third of this) and four yards in height.[14] The American artist complemented this with a commentary on the scenes. Other panoramas included poetry readings and appropriate music. For instance, a panorama that illustrated the overland route to India with contributions from the renowned Scottish watercolourist David Roberts attracted a quarter of a million visitors and was enhanced by the very professional narration of Joachim Heyward Stocqueler.[15]

However, the 'Panorama of the Nile' at the Egyptian Hall Piccadilly claimed a 'first': not only was it a moving diorama, but it was painted on transparent screens, which gave the audience the sensation that they were gliding gently up river on the west bank and, after the intermission, down the opposite bank. It included such wonders as torchlight views of the interior of the great temple at Abu Simbel and a representation of a camel caravan being lethally overtaken by a sandstorm.[16] This was just what the fans of Egyptian history and the 'sacred river' wanted, and on the opening night the eminent Syro-Egyptian Society visited the exhibition *en bloc*. The entertainment was presented at various venues from its opening in July 1849 until 1852, with pauses to allow for repainting and additions.

To ensure that the audiences got their money's worth – the admission fee was a mere shilling – the American promoters produced a handbook by the archaeologist John Gliddon, which described the 'Programme of the Grand Moving Panorama Picture of the Nile' as being some 800 feet in length and eight feet in height. It included all the features of interest over 1,720 miles of river from Cairo to the Second Cataract of Nubia, painted in 1849 from the original drawings of Joseph Bononi. The show was a spectacular success and the handbook quotes glowing press reports from a number of prestigious London journals and newspapers. *Punch,* however, was inclined to poke fun. On 14 July 1849, under the heading 'The Monster Panorama Manias', it stated:

> we can fancy one of [the artists] mounted on a camel, the camel's hair being from time to time cut to replenish the brushes, while the hump of the brute might be converted into a sort of easel very easily... we ought to take into consideration the courage of the artists in exploring such a river as the Nile, and looking all its perilous features in the face, particularly when some of those features include the mouth and teeth of that dental phenomenon – whom we should not like to encounter accidentally – the crocodile.

The handbook to the panorama included notes on the geography of the Nile, its geology and its historic monuments. Exactly how Selim became associated with this 'London sensation' in the heart of the metropolis is not known, but there is no reason to disbelieve him when he says: 'I... was obliged to take an engagement at the Egyptian Hall, Piccadilly, where I lectured on the Panorama of the Nile for nearly twelve months.'[17] Although it is not known whether he was referring to Selim, one German visitor praised the accompanying lecture

Egyptian Hall, Piccadilly, London (Museum of London)

as ‘full, lucid, and interesting.’[18] This presents an astonishing scenario. Here is a young black man, probably no more than 23 years old, taken from one of the most remote villages of the Sudan fourteen years previously and then plucked from slavery in Cairo, talking eloquently to large audiences from London society about the splendours of the Nile. We know from Burton that Selim had a pronounced Scottish accent, but this does not seemed to have affected his success. As an indigenous ‘Nilotic’ with experience as a slave on that river, Selim would have been a considerable draw for audiences. It would be surprising if he was not encouraged to relate his own remarkable story. That

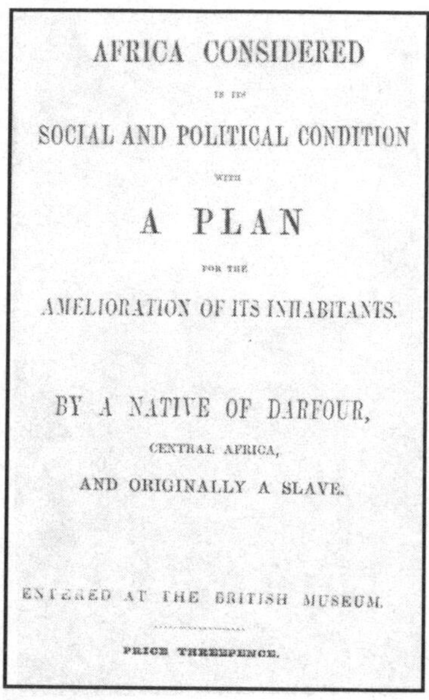

AFRICA CONSIDERED

IN ITS

SOCIAL AND POLITICAL CONDITION

WITH

A PLAN

FOR THE

AMELIORATION OF ITS INHABITANTS.

BY A NATIVE OF DARFOUR,

CENTRAL AFRICA,

AND ORIGINALLY A SLAVE.

ENTERED AT THE BRITISH MUSEUM.

PRICE THREEPENCE.

story, as described in his narrative of his early years, included a number of references to the treasures of the Nile which he had gleaned both from his trip with Robert Thurburn from Alexandria and from his use of the grand library at Murtle. Authenticity was all, and his very presence would have made up for any minor deficiencies in historical accuracy; the fact that he lectured for a year is testimony to his success. It would also have greatly increased his confidence. In his 1853 pamphlet, he gives one of his contact addresses as 'Panorama of the Slave Trade', suggesting that he might have gone on to be a lecturer on this topic also. No other reference to this panorama has been found, but the fact that its location is not specified suggests that it might have been too well known and advertised to require this.

A whole number of questions are raised by the abbreviated references in the pamphlet, and indeed the publication itself. Where did the funds come from for its printing and publication? Was the 'African Amelioration Society' Selim's own brainchild, and was it supported by others? The Society is described as having being established for 'the Cultivation of Free Grown Cotton' – in contradistinction to the crops grown by slave labour in the American plantations which formed the basis for the huge British trade in manufactured cottons. Selim asks for subscriptions but it is not known whether he received any. (As late as 1877 there

AFRICAN AMELIORATION SOCIETY,

ESTABLISHED FOR THE

CULTIVATION OF FREE GROWN COTTON,

JUNE, 1853.

SUBSCRIPTIONS RECEIVED BY SELIM AGA,

11, BREWER STREET, GOLDEN SQUARE, LONDON,

OR AT THE

PANORAMA OF THE SLAVE TRADE

1 JY 53

John K. Chapman and Company, 5 Shoe-lane, and Peterborough-court, Fleet-street.

Opposite: title page of Selim 's pamphlet prepared for the Foreign Office, 1853.
Above: an advert for the African Amelioration Society
(British Library)

is a record of a meeting of the 'good and great' in the Mansion House in London to plan for the civilisation of Africa through the ending of the slave trade; the large silver platter placed at the exit for donations contained a single shilling!)[19]

Selim's plan is full of high-flown rhetoric about the condition of Africa and the need for the civilisation of its inhabitants; what is surprising, is how little detail is provided on how this was to be achieved, besides the building of the trans-continental railway, no doubt with other people's money:

> A railway formed across Africa... will secure the trade of China, the East Indian Archipelago, India, Ceylon, and Arabia. It will save a sea voyage of seven thousand miles round the Cape of Good Hope... Imagine to yourself

> the pleasing prospect of seeing the inhabitants of Galla, Abyssinia, Darfur, Bornou, Houssa and of the Eboe countries, crowding to their respective Railway Stations to exchange the natural products of Africa, such as cotton, indigo, palm oil, ivory, and dyewoods, for Manchester prints and British cutlery... This plan would even become beneficial to emigrants going to Australia, for they could effect their transit in six weeks instead of four months.[20]

He was not to know that fifteen years later, in 1869, this purpose would be served by the cutting of the Suez Canal by Ferdinand de Lesseps. Selim himself is in no doubt about the degradation of his compatriots or what their salvation would mean for humanity:

> As central Africa may be considered the headquarters of ignorance and superstition, an idea will naturally suggest itself to the reader that the educating of its inhabitants will be a key to the civilisation of the whole world.[21]

Was his plan simply pigeonholed by the Foreign Office, as seems likely? More importantly, what did Selim do thereafter? According to Burton, he had offered to search for the papers of the German explorer Dr Vogel, who was murdered in Wadai, but was turned down in favour of the Scottish surgeon, William Baikie. It appears that Selim had made this application to Sir Roderick Murchison, then President of the Royal Geographical Society – who seems initially to have been in favour of his proposals – and it is likely that he did this while still in London. We do know, however, that he joined the official Niger Expedition of 1857 as a steward to the naval surveyor Lieutenant Glover.

CHAPTER NINE
Exploring the Niger

Know, Commerce follows nature's social laws,
As peace or charity her blessing draws –
Still shall she bear from Afric's genial plains
Their native wealth, though man untouched remains;
She hides no dagger in her flowing vest,
But frankly comes, caressing and caress't.

IN THE LATTER half of the eighteenth and the first half of the nineteenth centuries, the course of the great rivers of both East and West Africa remained a conundrum and Europeans became obsessed with finding the sources of the Nile, the Niger and the Congo. From earliest times parts of these rivers had been explored, and as long ago as the twelfth century the Moorish geographer El Adrisi correctly claimed that the Niger flowed into the Atlantic (but wrongly stated that it arose from the same source as the Nile). In the mid-fourteenth century, the indefatigable Arab traveller Ibn-Batuta explored this great West African river. He was followed in the early sixteenth century by the Spaniard Leo Africanus, in the course of writing his great work, *History and Description of Africa*.[1]

Many of these early writers thought that the Niger, arising in what was then the huge territory of the 'Soudan', flowed east and thence into the Nile. The Portuguese explorer Alvisi de Ca'da Mosto was among those who confused the river with the Senegal. The Scot Mungo Park, who explored the Niger region between 1795 and 1805, added greatly to knowledge of the river. He died in 1805 at Bussa on the Niger in a presumed ambush, one of many Europeans whose venture into this hostile and disease-ridden environment cost them their lives.[2] Only five of the forty-four Europeans who accompanied him on his second and final expedition survived. His countryman Hugh Clapperton died at Sokoto in 1827, without having discovered the source of the river. Uncertainty about the true course of the Niger remained until the early 1830s, when the Lander brothers, Richard and John, finally established it by travelling its length, to its outlet on the Atlantic.[3] From 1795 to 1855, Europeans attempted no less than thirteen journeys of discovery around this river.

Considerable impetus was given to its exploration by the

establishment of the Association for Promoting the Discovery of the Interior Parts of Africa in London in 1788, largely the creation of Sir Joseph Banks, who had, as a young man, made his name as Cooke's botanist on the *Endeavour* and who achieved the distinction of becoming President of the prestigious Royal Society at the age of thirty-five. The Association was to become the Geographical Society and subsequently, in 1831, the Royal Geographical Society. Until slavery was 'abolished' in the British Empire in 1838, West Africa had been the happy hunting ground for slavers, who exported vast human cargoes to the plantations of the Americas; for most of the eighteenth century, the relationship between Europe, especially Britain, and this part of Africa was dominated by the trade. There was a certain awful symmetry between the guns and cheap goods supplied by Britain to pay for slaves whose labours in the plantation fields sent cotton and sugar back to Britain. European commercial interests and local chiefs alike were engaged in this trade and were wary of any possible interference in their nefarious activities, effectively discouraging more altruistic scientific exploration.

British abolitionists argued that the slave trade could be replaced by legitimate commerce, combined with the spreading of the Christian message. This concept was actively supported by philanthropic entrepreneurs and businessmen, including the Liverpool shipbuilder Macgregor Laird, owner of the African Steamship Company. Laird saw the commercial potential in opening up the Niger to steamship trade, not least for the expansion of the palm oil industry. He also saw the possibility of circumventing the import to Britain of slave-grown cotton from America by favouring cotton grown in Africa.

In 1832, an expedition up the Niger led by Macgregor Laird and Richard Lander, in two boats, ended in disaster. Only nine out of the forty-nine Europeans who had left England survived. Most had succumbed to disease, while Lander died from gunshot wounds. A second attempt was made in 1841 with three ships, a white crew of 135 men and an equal number of black seamen. It was even more of a failure than that of ten years earlier.

One of the major players on the stage of West African exploration was the German explorer Heinrich Barth. In five years he would travel over 10,000 miles and become unequalled as an African explorer, surpassing even Livingstone, though without the latter's fame.[4] Barth started out from England in 1849 and reached the Niger in June 1853, having confirmed that the river did not arise in Lake Chad, as commonly supposed. Concern about his long absence without communication resulted in his compatriot German Dr Edward Vogel being sent out from England in February 1853 to ascertain his whereabouts.[5] Meanwhile Barth had reached Timbuctoo, where he was kept a virtual prisoner for over eight months. Here he learned of Vogel's relief expedition and, more by good luck than planning, encountered his rescuer on 1 December 1854. After some time together, Vogel continued on his explorations south-east of Lake Chad but was subsequently murdered in January 1855 under circumstances which have never been resolved. Barth returned safely to England in September 1855. To his considerable chagrin, he found that his old friend Dr William Baikie, in the course of his expedition up the Niger in 1854, had been asked to make contact with him and to ascertain the fate of Dr Vogel.

Selim was to become involved both with the search for Dr Vogel, and then with Baikie in his second expedition up the Niger in 1857. In *Abeokuta and the Camaroons Mountains: An Exploration*, Burton states that Selim 'returned to Africa in 1857 with that failure of failures, the Niger expedition'. In the

Geographic Magazine of 1875, Burton makes a further reference but appears to make an error in the date, when he says:

> In 1860 [Selim] returned to his natal continent, after volunteering personally to ascertain the facts concerning the murder, in Waday, of Dr Vogel, attached to the Central African Expedition. The late Sir Roderick Murchison and others were favourable to the plan, but they at length determined that all measures should be left in the hands of the late Dr Baikie.[6]

At another point in the same narrative Burton says, 'In 1860 Selim Aga proposed to recover the papers of the late Dr Vogel... Dr Baikie, chief of the Niger expedition, proposed to do this himself. So Selim was thrown out, and Dr Baikie has not yet done it' – a typically waspish Burton remark, to diminish explorers other than himself, with the implication that Selim was quite up to the job had it not been for the preferences of the British geographical establishment.[7]

It appears most unlikely, considering Selim's lack of credentials with that establishment, that he would have been given command of anything resembling an official expedition to investigate Dr Vogel's disappearance or to recover his papers, although a proposal to conduct a private search, trading on Selim's ethnic background and language skills, may have been looked upon with favour. To understand these somewhat confusing references to an association between Selim and Baikie, it is necessary to look at the background to Baikie's two expeditions up the Niger.

William Balfour Baikie, born in Orkney in 1825, studied medicine in Edinburgh, and there took a great interest in natural history. In 1848 he joined the Royal Navy as an assistant

Dr William Balfour Baikie
(Trustees of the National Library of Scotland)

surgeon, serving on a number of ships before being posted to Haslar Hospital where the great geologist and geographer Sir Roderick Murchison was superintendent. Murchison encouraged the young naval surgeon to apply to accompany yet another expedition up the Niger, led by the experienced British Consul at Fernando Po, John Beecroft.[8] However, by the time Baikie reached Fernando Po in June 1854 in the iron-screw steamer *Pleiad*, Beecroft had died. As the next most senior officer, Baikie had to assume command – a considerable challenge for the young surgeon, inexperienced as he was. He took on Beecroft's remit to investigate the potential of the Niger for trade and proselytising purposes, to offer assistance to Dr Barth and to enquire into the fate of Dr Vogel. Despite problems with the captain of the *Pleiad*, Baikie led the expedition courageously and skilfully. Unusually in the depressing annals of exploration in this region, he returned within sixteen months without the loss of a single life.[9]

Apart from navigating and recording scientific data along 700 miles of river, 250 miles further than had previously been reached, his most important contribution to exploration and future settlement in West Africa was his use of daily doses of quinine to combat malaria and other fevers: Baikie had insisted that all aboard the *Pleiad* take a daily dose of six or eight grams

Lieutenant John Glover, RN (Trustees of the National Library of Scotland)

dissolved in sherry.[10] The efficacy of this treatment changed the whole prospect of development and trade in the area. He was unable to make contact with Dr Barth, who by this time was on his return journey to Tripoli, or to find out anything concerning the fate of Dr Vogel, although he was able to recover two of Dr Vogel's books in Kano in 1862.

One of those who made a signal contribution to the success of this expedition was the Reverend Samuel Crowther, who had been on the 1832 expedition under Macgregor Laird and Richard Lander. Baikie makes fulsome acknowledgement of Crowther in correspondence and even Burton, usually contemptuous of missionaries, admired this black churchman. Crowther was enslaved at the age of eleven, but the ship carrying him to the Cuban plantations was intercepted by a vessel of the British West African Squadron and he was brought to Sierra Leone, the British colony for liberated slaves. He subsequently became the first Bishop of the Niger, translating the Bible into several local languages; this linguistic ability was immensely useful to Baikie on both his expeditions. Crowther was consulted on matters of expedition policy and was often the chief negotiator with local tribes. His journals contributed greatly to an understanding of the peoples along this great waterway, and this knowledge provided a basis for the establishment of the first Christian missions there.

Neither Baikie's narrative of the 1854 expedition nor that of Crowther makes any reference to Selim and so it may be assumed that he was not one of that company.[11] There are references to 'Selim' from at least two different sources in the accounts of Baikie's 1857 expedition, one by Crowther and the other by Lieutenant John Glover, as reported by his biographer, ACG Hastings. The purpose of this expedition was to make accurate charts of the river and to establish trading posts and mission settlements. Again it was Macgregor Laird's company that supplied the main vessel, the *Dayspring* (and its supply ship, the *George*), which arrived at the island of Fernando Po on 29 June 1857. Unlike previous paddle steamers, the *Dayspring* was specially constructed to navigate the Niger, with shallow draft and screw propulsion. Glover was the expedition's surveyor and specimen collector; other specialists included a surgeon, a botanist and a zoologist.

Glover had been in the Royal Navy since the age of twelve and had seen service in West Africa, the Baltic and Burma. It is clear that he was courageous and determined: Hastings implies that he, rather than Baikie, was the effective leader of the expedition.[12] (He would later be appointed as the first Governor of Lagos.) However, by the end of the seven-week journey from England in the cramped quarters of the *Dayspring,* which was never intended for regular ocean-going, he was heartily sick of the voyage, although he busied himself by reading accounts of earlier explorers such as Burton, Barth and Denham.[13]

At Fernando Po, they spent a week ashore making preparations for the journey, and were joined by the African missionaries Samuel Crowther and John Taylor, both of whom impressed Glover. Given that Crowther's single reference to Selim is as Glover's servant, it is interesting that an Englishman called Fisher is designated in the same capacity by Hastings, who also describes a certain Fulani and Arabic scholar as a very faithful servant to the lieutenant. Hastings refers to Selim as 'an interpreter', which suggests he had been in the country long enough to enable him to learn something of the local languages.

By 3 July, with the supply ship lashed to the *Dayspring,* the expedition arrived at the Brass River, halting at each of the villages *en route* in order to contact with local people and to allow Crowther to attempt some missionary work. The journey through the swamps of the delta had been plagued by sand flies and mosquitoes. The dense mangroves, with their mass of upright roots reaching out of the water, created an impassable barrier for vessels, which had to follow any natural openings to find a route; the innumerable creeks presented considerable navigation challenges.

At Igbobi, the chief indicated that he would be glad to have a trading station at his village. At Abo, despite being presented with a cocked hat and a red umbrella, the chief, Aje, demanded the offer of more and more presents, which he simply took if he fancied them.[14] Taylor and thirteen others were left behind to establish a mission station and school at Onitsha, at the junction of the Benue and the Niger. Crowther was constantly on the lookout for opportunities for settlement along the river, while Glover marked the villages and any other prominent features on his charts. He was surveying from dawn to dusk, having his food brought to him. On Sundays, however, there was a full church service with communion. Glover was not impressed, on this single day of rest, by Baikie's exhortations to push forward.

By 7 August they had reached Idda, where another mission was proposed. In addition to ivory, there was plentiful local produce including cotton, palm oil, tobacco, pepper, rice, Indian corn, yams, goats, sheep and fowls, all of which augured well for future trade. Here too there was ample evidence of the continuing slave trade (the price was about £7 for a woman with a child), while the king had his retinue of eunuchs.[15]

The *George,* with its cargo of trading merchandise, was left behind at the confluence of the Niger and Tshaddda, at Idda, freeing the *Dayspring* to proceed up river without this burden. But the expedition was ill-starred. There were outbreaks of fever and sometimes hostile receptions from the locals: the second-in-command, May, refused to take orders, while the crew complained about their treatment at the hands of Captain Grant, the bullying shipmaster, and Berwick, the surgeon.[16] Baikie was obliged to report this conduct to Lord Clarendon at the Foreign Office. Morale was not helped by the death of Rees, the mate, in September.

Disaster struck on 7 October, just past the township of Rabba. Crowther describes the wrecking of the expedition vessel on the notorious ju-ju rock near Jebba:

> The true passage being doubtful, the ship was stopped and Lieut. Glover went to sound, first the creek, then the passages between the rocks... it was calculated that the *Dayspring* would be able to pass with her full power... for a few minutes the ship was put to her right course at half her speed, then with her full power of 120 revolutions; but she could not keep up. She was drifted a little, and struck her head upon her port bow. The engine was stopped for a moment to allow her to drop down a little, when she was started again with her full power. For a few moments she stood steadily before she recovered herself, and made head fairly. By this time the current and eddy caught her on the port side, and there being about ten or fifteen feet more to clear out of this narrow channel, or sixty yards in breadth, she was drifted on to the sunken rocks in the bed of the river, on her starboard side, where she remained fast and steady, and soon began to make water in the engine room and in the aft cabin. The pumps were set to work, and immediate measures taken to heave her off, and to put to the nearest sandbank on shore.[17]

All efforts to save the boat failed. During this incident both the captain and Glover were sick, vomiting all day.[18] Glover and another crew member, Mackintosh, were the last to leave the stricken vessel. The twelve Europeans and thirty-eight blacks sheltered from the torrential rain on a sandbank as best they could. They had been able to salvage very little from their vessel; it went down with most of its stores, specimens, survey data and rations. Baikie and Glover had lost their clothes, books and instruments. In the weeks that followed, morale plummeted further and there was virtual mutiny among the crew, which

The *Dayspring* (Trustees of the National Library of Scotland)

was only suppressed by a show of arms. Things got to such a pitch that the ringleaders had to be sent down to Lairdstown to await the arrival of the relief ship, the *Sunbeam*. Hating inactivity, the energetic Glover, with Baikie's permission, set off on 16 November on an exploration of the higher reaches of the river. After many adventures by canoe and horseback (the latter having been lent by local chiefs), his party succeeded in reaching the township of Bussa, where Mungo Park died. Here they were very well received by the chief and his people. To reach Bussa alone was a very considerable achievement: in doing so, they had travelled further up the Niger – a distance of 700 miles – than any Europeans previously.[19]

They returned to the main camp at Jebba on 5 January 1858

after an absence of fifty-two days, to find the expedition in an even more demoralised state. There was no news of the *Sunbeam*, rations were dangerously low, and they had nothing to offer by way of trade for food. Baikie had decided against proceeding to his destination at Sokoto. After another journey to Bussa to advise the chief there that the party would have to defer its visit, Glover rejoined the main expedition on 4 February; according to Burton, Selim had accompanied the party. Here Glover's journal ends, but it is known from Crowther's record, and confirmed by Hastings, that Glover travelled overland to Sierra Leone and Lagos to get help, accompanied by Selim.[20] According to Crowther: 'This afternoon (February 15th) Lieutenant Glover, with Selim his servant, left the camp for Lagos, on their way to Sierra Leone.' On 20 May he was to report: 'Lieutenant Glover arrived from Lagos, having been to Sierra Leone and back: he brought supplies for the expedition, and a box for me from Mr Taylor.'[21]

This journey was a remarkable feat, covering several hundred miles from Jebba, through difficult territory, to Ibadan. It would have taxed even Selim's considerable survival skills; additionally, Glover was laid up for a time with acute dysentery. Selim, in his early thirties, would have been about the same age as Glover, but there is no indication of what their personal relationship was, although Burton's later comments suggest that Glover respected Selim for his loyalty and practical skills. In his *Wanderings in West Africa* Burton states that Glover, 'by means of his steward, Selim Agha, returned overland to Lagos'. At Lagos, a ship was obtained to take them to Sierra Leone, the only place where the necessary stores could be obtained. In contradiction to Burton, Lady Glover's account of her husband's life suggests that it was only in Sierra Leone that Lieut. Glover 'made the acquaintance of Selim Oga [*sic*] an African, who had gained some little reputation for himself'. The misspelling of his name and slightly patronising reference to Selim casts doubt on the accuracy of this.

They had further hair-raising adventures when Glover took some former Hausa slaves back to Lagos and their enraged owners attempted to recapture them – with Glover himself only escaping by the skin of his teeth.[22] After delivering his stores to Jebba, he returned to Lagos to pilot the *Sunbeam* upriver when the waters were deep enough for its draught, to reach the Jebba camp after the expedition had been benighted there for over a year. The party reached Fernando Po on 8 November 1858.

Contrary to what Burton says, this journey, in the longer term, was not a disaster. It had very important consequences for the future trading development of West Africa. The use of quinine meant that only one man died on the expedition. It opened up the prospect of using the river as a trading artery with a journey of only fourteen days from Benue to Kano, the most important market city in West Africa, compared to the fourteen months trek along the traditional overland route from Tripoli in North Africa.

The river having been made safe, the British forsook the long and much more difficult route from North Africa and used its naval power to secure virtually exclusive entry into the interior via the Niger – an important element in the subsequent partition and exploitation of West African territories. Baikie returned to the trading settlement at the confluence with the Benue, remaining there as consul for the rest of his life and thus becoming the first British settler and civil servant in what was to become the great nation of Nigeria.[23] Selim had played a not insignificant part, not least in the rescue of the party, in one of the most important explorations on the continent.

CHAPTER TEN

‘He took all the trouble of life off my hands’

Thus lived the Negro in his native land,
Till Christian cruisers anchor'd on his strand;
Where'er their grasping arms the spoilers spread,
The Negro's joys, the Negro's virtues fled.

BETWEEN 1861 AND 1864, Selim was to be closely associated with one of the most remarkable characters of the Victorian age: Richard Francis Burton. There are at least ten biographies of Burton. Most of them conclude that his personality was so complex as to defy definition, particularly as he himself laid so many false trails. Born in 1821, he was introduced to travel at an early age as the son of an Army colonel, and in adult years never seemed able to settle down in any one place for any length of time. Following expulsion from Oxford University for attending horse-racing, he joined the army of the East India Company aged twenty-one and achieved the rank of captain.

Physically he was very robust and he was a renowned swordsman; allied to a formidable constitution was an intellect regarded as one of the keenest of the age. With an extraordinary memory and gift of imitation, he mastered twenty-five languages and was proficient in almost as many dialects. He was a pioneer in anthropology, a lifetime interest. He was an outstanding oriental scholar, which, together with a penchant for disguise, enabled him to penetrate different cultures. Famously, he journeyed to the forbidden city of Mecca disguised as a travelling Arab doctor. As a writer he could be incisive and colourful, or obscure and digressive, confusing the reader with parenthetical observations which might be only marginally relevant to his subject.[1]

In his attitudes towards other nationalities or races, for which he has been severely criticised, some have argued that he was no worse than many of the age – but few, if any, gave vent to their prejudices so vituperatively or arrogantly as Burton did. A reviewer said of him:

> Captain Burton, who knows our 'black brother' to the backbone, shows us behind the scenes. He regards him

> as a provisional creature who has his day, and who will then pass away according to the programme, and clear the ground 'for higher successors'... if there is any hope for the African, and if he is to advance a single step, Captain Burton thinks it will be through Muhammedanism... There is only one serious drawback, and it will be considered overwhelming – Muslims will not become Christians.[2]

The last remark must be the opinion of the reviewer and not that of Burton, who was barely even a nominal Christian and was contemptuous of missionaries. He was an intemperate man to the point of being quite outrageous in his insensitivity towards others, although he himself did not take kindly to criticism. He was impatient with bureaucracy, routine and convention, and enjoyed his reputation for shocking delicate Victorian sensibilities, particularly through his almost obsessive interest in eroticism and the sexual behaviour of

Richard Burton in his tent in Africa (Trustees of the National Library of Scotland)

native peoples. Allied to this seems to have been an unhealthy interest in cruel practices, such as human sacrifice, mutilation and cannibalism – any activity which would be regarded as 'beyond the pale'. He did in fact go to some lengths to establish a sinister reputation, although perhaps this was yet another of his disguises.

This extraordinary man achieved much less than his potential would suggest. He was a deeply flawed individual, who, despite his dissimulation, was perhaps subconsciously attempting to establish an identity. Unfortunately this was too often at the expense of others and his undoubted talents and achievements were overshadowed by a capacity for waywardness amounting to self-destruction. Although he was knighted in 1866, no one could accuse him of being an example of the British establishment, with his contempt for almost all official institutions and their mores.

By the time he met Selim, Burton had already lived several lives – as a soldier in India and in the Crimea, as the adventurer who had penetrated the dangerous cities of Mecca and Harar in disguise, as the explorer who had made the epic journey to Lake Tanganyika with Speke in the search for the source of the Nile, and as the writer and poet who was known for his scholarly translations of oriental literature. The reviewer quoted above, perhaps somewhat ironically, put his finger on Burton's quicksilver theatricality:

> If Captain Burton is not actually before the public, he has always got irons in the fire, is always preparing dashing surprises, and never fails to astonish the community either by his feats as a traveller or by the variety and unequalled extent of his knowledge and acquirements.

Burton married in 1861. His wife Isabel had expensive tastes and he badly needed a secure income, which propelled him to seek a post with the Foreign Office, against his instinctive inclinations. In September of that year he was appointed British Consul in Fernando Po, a small mountainous island under Spanish control some nineteen miles off the West African coast. The island was known as a lethal posting, the graveyard of Europeans consigned there, at least at lower, mosquito-ridden altitudes. It is dominated by Clarence Peak, rising to almost 4,000 metres, which in Burton's day was still clothed with luxuriant indigenous forest like much of the rest of the island. This forest provided sanctuary for the aboriginal inhabitants, who had an unsavoury reputation, mostly unfounded. Wherever the forest was cleared for agriculture, its rich soils and moist climate yielded bountiful crops of tropical fruits, coffee, cocoa and sugar cane. Burton, who clearly hated Fernando Po – 'the very abomination of desolation' – regarded this base as merely a jumping-off point for his own personal and idiosyncratic explorations into the interior of West Africa. He had frequent jousts with the Foreign Office about trips which were unrelated to his consular duties and taken without official permission. (His expenses of £43 for a journey up the Congo were refused on the grounds that this was outside his district.) There were also complaints about the fact that his reports were written in minute, almost indecipherable script.[3]

Within a week of arrival at his consular station, he had taken the opportunity of a passage in a naval ship to Lagos, with the intention of travelling into the previously unexplored Cameroon Mountains via Abeokuta, the capital of the powerful Yoruba people. It was here that he recruited Selim as his manservant, or, as he usually called him, his 'factotum'. There is no indication

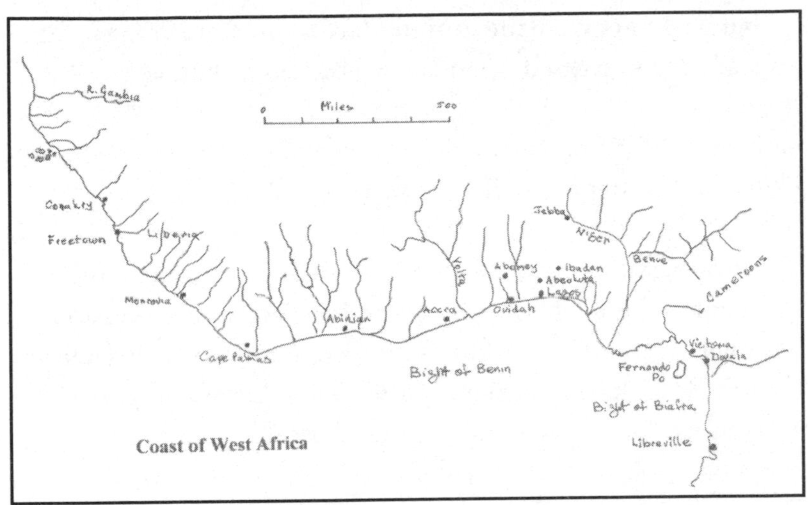

The coast of West Africa (James McCarthy)

of how he found Selim, but it is more than likely that Selim was recommended by someone for whom he had previously worked, possibly in the consulate. It is not unlikely that Burton would have recruited Selim on the strength of his previous connection with the Thurburns. With his knowledge of the Thurburns and other European travellers such as Baikie, Selim would have been aware of the opportunities provided by official representatives, and his fluent English is likely to have stood him in good stead. Burton is generous in his praise of Selim, which says a great deal, given Burton's critical attitude, not least towards Africans. In his record of the exploration of the Cameroon Mountains, he claims that Selim:

> proved himself perfection; a Figaro, but un-Figaro-like –honest, civil, unpresuming: he could cook, doctor, shave, valet, garden, carpenter, shoot and stuff birds, collect spirit specimens – in fact he took all the trouble of life off my

> hands. I at once made him my factotum, regretting to see such a man wasted upon the barbarism of Lagos.

In his published works Burton gives many instances of Selim's skills, and courage, predicting that:

> Some years hence, when we shall have topographical engineers, and when exploration shall become a profession, not as at present, an affair of mere amateurship, Selim Agas will be useful in cutting a path for the European pioneer through Outer Asia and Central Africa.[4]

Burton clearly sees 'European pioneers' as the civilising agents, but with the Selim Agas of this world as the frontier scouts. Given Burton's frequently aired prejudices, Selim would have commended himself to him by the simple fact of not having 'negroid' features. Burton describes his physical characteristics in the *Geographical Magazine* of 1 July 1875:

> Selim Agha did not belong to the Guinea Coast, or the Congo people, most familiar to Europe and to the Southern States of North America; he boasted of the old semi-Semitic Abyssinian blood, in former times mixed, doubtless, with that of the half-Arab Bedawin who still feed their flocks near the western shores of the Red Sea... Physically, he was a type of the mixed race. With short curly hair, and coal-black skin, his head and face as far as the nostrils were distinctly Arab; the rest was as clearly African. His thin and sinewy limbs were those of the Berber, whilst the feet and hands suggested the Mswahili. Such are the men who prove how much can be done for the African by

> good European training, and who, like the 'Pundits' lately known to fame, can freely penetrate into the central parts of Nigerland, so dangerous, if not deadly, to white men. And these are the races who, extending southwards, with slow but regular advance, will, after many generations, mix their blood with the tribes typified by the Congo; will spread Islamism through the 'Heart of Africa,' and will pave the way for a higher civilization.[5]

There is an implication here that Selim was a Muslim, but elsewhere in the same letter Burton refers to him as being 'strongly affected towards Presbyterianism', which is not unlikely given his experience in north-east Scotland. Selim's own writings from his time at Murtle indicate that he was a committed Christian.

Selim was considered by Burton as an exemplary jack-of-all-trades and, perhaps most importantly, he did not display the 'insolence' which Burton attributed to many part-educated West Africans. In his *Geographic Magazine* article quoted above, Burton refers to Selim as his *compagnon de voyage,* and it would appear that this is no mere turn of phrase; throughout three years of travel in West Africa, Selim was by Burton's side; in storms on board ship, at meetings with surly chiefs, on climbs up unscaled mountains and in bringing rebellious porters to heel. In the many fraught situations in which Burton found himself, especially in his altercations with rapacious petty chiefs who tried his patience to the limit, Selim was clearly a rock on whom Burton depended. There would have been many occasions, in the absence of European company, when Burton would have looked to Selim for a modicum of civilised companionship and support, quite distinct from the usual master-servant relationship. On his last journey in West Africa, to Dahomey, Burton states that he was alone: 'in such matters negroes do not count as men'.[6] Despite his high opinion of Selim, who accompanied him, he was not regarded in the same way as a European companion.

The records of the expeditions on which Selim accompanied Burton are largely contained in official reports or published narratives and provide scant information on the daily routines, the equipment carried, or their domestic arrangements. Nevertheless, much of this can be inferred from other explorations of the time and the advice given by, for example, the Royal Geographical Society in their *Hints for Travellers*. Burton was one of the last of the 'romantic' explorers, impatient with the tedious routines of route surveying and mapping; indeed, few if any of his journeys in West Africa could be considered exploratory in any original sense. He seems to have disdained mere delineation of the landscape in favour of a more literary approach. Above all, he was fascinated by anthropological curiosities and recorded customs in minute detail. There are no references to taking astronomical observations or boiling thermometers to determine altitudes, although this would have been done in the Cameroon Mountains. Nor does Burton make much reference to the fitting out required for any journey in Africa, which was always laborious and time-consuming.

There was the recruitment of porters and headmen, establishing their contracts, rates of pay and rations – often little more than two cupfuls of rice, given out at the end of the day. After the first few days, until they reached native settlements, the caravan would be dependent on local food sources which had to be negotiated with chiefs, only some of whom were cooperative. Even where they were, they inevitably saw this as an opportunity to raise 'prices' in the form of presents. As much as two thirds of the loads carried into the interior consisted of cloths, beads, wire and items to be used in barter and to satisfy the demands of all and sundry who laid claim on the travellers. At each stage, careful calculations had to be made regarding the supplies that would be required to see the men to the end of the expedition. Horses and canoes could sometimes be hired at the rate of about nine shillings per day, or its equivalent in cowrie shells, cloth, etc. While a large caravan could carry more of these trade goods, the additional porters would themselves require food, and so there had to be a carefully balanced calculation of requirements.

Burton frequently describes his problems with recalcitrant porters who were not averse to blackmail in their demands for increased pay, with their refusals to proceed, persistent pilfering of stores, drunkenness and actual desertion. While Burton's authoritarian approach, floggings and armed threats may have been effective on some occasions, he seems to have encountered more problems in this respect than other travellers: later, for example, the Scots explorer Joseph Thomson was to prove equally if not more effective using much more diplomatic methods.

Keeping the porters in order and maintaining their morale in the face of often trying circumstances was crucial, and Europeans came to realise the value of a disciplined African headman or caravan leader. Keith Johnston, on his fateful 1879 expedition with Joseph Thomson, extolled the virtues in this respect of Livingstone's old servant Chuma.[7] What was required was the equivalent of a sergeant-major, and Burton seems to have found this in Selim, to whom he frequently delegated the business of ensuring that the porters and their burdens got to their daily destinations, while he himself marched on ahead. Dependent on the terrain and their loads, the porters would not be able to exceed twelve miles per day.

The porters' loads ranged from sixty to eighty pounds, usually carried on the head, often with considerable fighting between the men at the start of the day as to who should carry which, the hard-edged boxes of more delicate equipment being least favoured. The men themselves were provided with food and clothes suitable in Burton's view for higher altitudes and his list, with costs, for seven porters makes interesting reading:

		£	s	d
7	BLUE SHIRTS	2	5	6
7	SERGE TROUSERS	3	10	0
7	PRS BOOTS	3	10	0
12	RED WOOLLEN CAPS	0	6	0
2	DOZEN MATCHETS	0	1	0
2	HATCHETS	2	10	0
2	(WATER) BREAKERS	0	8	8
452	LBS RICE	7	10	8
200	LBS PORK	7	10	0
14½	GALLONS RUM	3	2	10
5	PIECES BLUE BAFT CLOTH	3	5	0
2	DITTO SATIN STRIPE	0	17	4
	TOTAL:	33	8	10

As his manservant, Selim was responsible for Burton's clothing and personal effects, including his weapons, and writing materials, such as powdered ink and his journal. Crucially, Selim would have been in charge of the medicine chest, of which the most important item was quinine, which had only lately proved to be an effective prophylactic against malaria, although the causes of that devastating disease were still unknown. Most of the other medicines were quite useless against scourges such as dysentery and yellow fever. It appears that Selim had some ability in general doctoring, which he may have learned at Murtle, and he would be constantly called upon by the porters, particularly for the treatment of leg ulcers, which were rife. Burton was required to keep a meticulous account of his expenses for the Foreign Office but clearly disliked this chore, which was delegated to Selim wherever possible. (In Burton's invoices to the Foreign Office there is a solitary record of the cost of Selim's board for ten days at £1.2s.6d. – alongside £7.17s.0d. for seven cases of gin!) One of Selim's special responsibilities was to check on the condition of the specimens of plants and birds, most of which he had personally skinned and stuffed, to be forwarded to the British Museum and Kew Gardens.

The travellers were usually up before sunrise to take advantage of the coolest part of the day. Selim would bring tea to Burton and hot water for shaving (Burton suggests that he was shaved by Selim). It was Selim who is likely to have cooked for Burton and other Europeans, using whatever local foodstuffs he could bargain for on their behalf. Again his experience at Murtle was valuable, as he had not only learnt to cook to suit European tastes (turtle soup was a speciality) but also to observe standards of hygiene and presentation, including the serving of drinks. He would ensure that Burton's clothes and boots were clean and laid out for each day's journey and that all his personal effects were carefully packed in their correct boxes and bundles.

It would take up to three hours to organise the porters with their loads ready for the march, particularly if the morning was wet and they were disinclined to get out of their night shelters. There would often be arguments with the guides as to the route and how far they could expect to travel, some of the men throwing down their loads to make clear their disgust at what was expected of them. Selim had his work cut out to keep the men together and to prevent pilfering. In terms of freeing Burton from all the practical chores of a caravan, Selim was worth his weight in gold, not least because of his energy and reliability.

Prior to his first expedition to the Cameroon Mountains with Commander Bedingfield and a Mr Eales, Burton spent several weeks during November 1861 at the Yoruba capital of Abeokuta. He makes typically caustic comments on Bedingfield's presumption of knowing all about African affairs and on Eales's belief in the occurrence in West Africa of unicorns, which he was now hunting.[8] Burton provides a detailed description of the town, its defensive position and the goods traded in its market; his account of this expedition is of a piece with his other writings, taking every opportunity to comment on the landscape, vegetation, natural history, settlements and anthropology of the local people, etc, digressing extensively into his favourite topics, such as disease, religion and the benefits of polygamy. However, attempting to find a route to the Ogun River through the impenetrable mangrove swamps, Burton states, 'Selim was the only one of the party who knew the way by experience, and with his aid, we shot into the Agboi Creek.'[9] There is no record of where Selim gained that experience, but it is likely to have been with a previous official expedition.

One of Burton's objects was to meet the King of Oyo to make formal representations on behalf of the British Government concerning the continuance of the slave trade and human sacrifices in his dominions. After delays and displays of aggression, a treaty, albeit a somewhat vague one, was drawn up to end these practices. The presentations at court were long-drawn-out ceremonial affairs, which Burton attempted to sketch. One of these sketches shows the king and his retinue, together

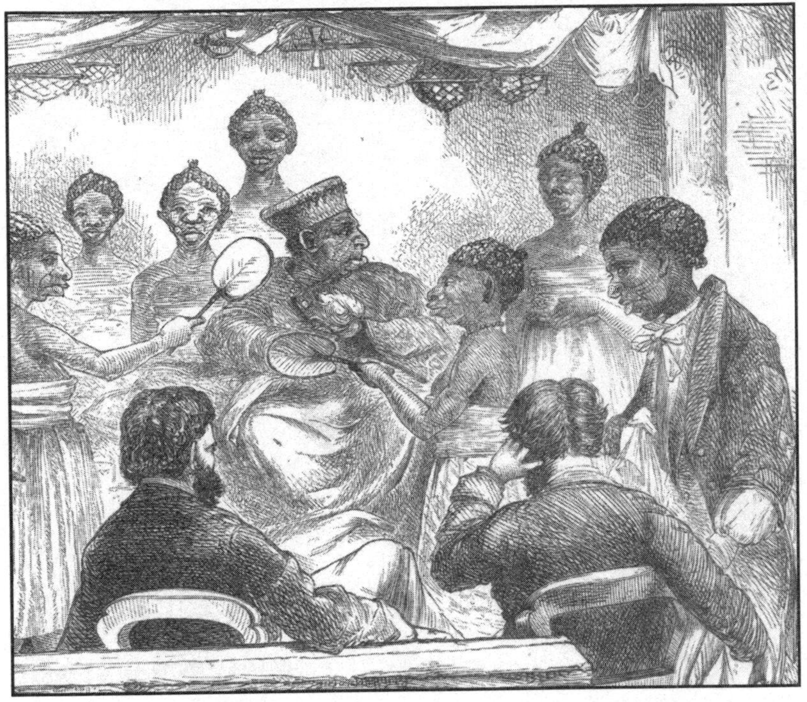

Presentation at the court of King Oyo – is this Selim on the right? (Trustees of the National Library of Scotland)

with the Europeans, and on the right hand side, an African in frock coat and white cravat, who may be Selim, or possibly the interpreter, Lagos Williams – Burton was known to dress up his retinue for formal appearances. If it is Selim, it would be the only known image of him. However, if the image has been redrawn by an artist other than Burton himself for purposes of book illustration, it may not represent a true likeness.[10]

CHAPTER ELEVEN
Selim Hoists the Union Jack

O'er the wild mountains and luxuriant plains
Nature in all the pomp of beauty reigns.

THE PARTY WHICH set out to the Cameroon Mountains in December 1861 comprised, apart from Burton and Selim, Atilano Calvo Iturburu, a Spanish judge from Fernando Po; the young Gustav Mann, a British government botanist in West Africa; and the local English missionary, the Reverend Alfred Saker, who was based at the fledgling mission station at Victoria and whose knowledge of the local people and their dialect was a particular asset. Mann had been with Baikie's 1859 expedition up the Niger, replacing the previous expedition botanist, Charles Baxter, who had tragically died, and gained rare praise from Burton for connecting local species to the flora of other distant regions of Africa. One of the main objectives was to be the first to climb the highest peaks of the Cameroons, and, following the establishment of Lagos as a British colony, Burton was also looking for possible sites for penal settlements and accessible locations at higher altitudes where sanatoria for Europeans suffering from malaria might be viable.[1]

Mann, a professional botanist intent on making comprehensive collections of native plants (he collected over 200 species), gave the expedition an overt scientific purpose. Burton himself collected many animal and bird specimens, which were sent to London for identification. These are listed in the published record of the expedition; several species were officially named after Burton's wife and one bird after Burton himself. Several were shot by Selim, who was responsible for stuffing the small mammals, which raises the question of where he learnt this specialist skill. When Mann was prostrated by illness, it was Selim, under Burton's supervision, who took the daily thermometric observations. It is clear from the upright and independent botanist's reports to the Director of Kew Gardens that Mann did not take kindly to being patronised by Burton, who – accustomed to being 'head man' – objected, in turn, to Mann carrying out explorations without his approval.[2] Towards the end of the expedition, when Burton had almost given up on finding concrete evidence of recent volcanic activity in the form of a 'solfaterra' or minor eruptions through rock fissures, it was Selim who discovered a source:

> accompanied by my factotum and a krooboy, I climbed up the dyke separating the two great chasms, and walked down a smooth cinder valley trending north-east... still disappointed I turned to the north-west, behind Albert Crater, and observed some suspicious cracks and gashes, long, narrow, and deep, which raised my hopes sky-high; they proved however, thoroughly extinct... Hardly had the candle been lighted when Selim, who had struck over certain dwarf and broken hillocks, stained with red and yellow, and lying due north of where I stood, re-appeared, highly excited. When he told me the cause, his feelings were shared; we started on grand gallop, and presently met our reward. My factotum had discovered a complete solfaterra... smoke arose in puffy volumes from the long lines of marl and sulphur... I am pleased to announce to the Royal Geographical Society of Great Britain the addition of another volcano, not wholly extinct, to the list of those already known.

The above information was published in the *Proceedings of the Royal Geographical Society* for 16 June 1863. It is to Burton's credit that he acknowledges the part played by Selim, whose contribution to the scientific achievements of the expedition he could so easily have omitted from the record.

Burton's party in the Cameroon Mountains
(Trustees of the National Library of Scotland)

Although Burton goes into ecstasies about the magnificence of the mountain landscape, the bracing air and the delights of the luxuriant tropical forest with its verdant ferneries, the actual ascent was a formidable physical challenge, considerably exacerbated by thieving porters who used every excuse to tarry, demanding more pay, or feigning injury. He describes his entourage as 'six men, under Black Will, a consummate ruffian. Despite however a sound preliminary dressing… and the vigorous applications of my excellent steward, Selim Aga, Will soon managed to sprain his ankle and to return to Victoria.'[3] Following a bout of pilfering from their tent, Selim was put in charge of the recalcitrant gang, with orders that no man should enter the tent or touch the rations.

In fact, it appears that throughout the expedition, Selim was made responsible for all of the Kru-men, as the porters were called, often being in sole charge when the unburdened

Europeans went on ahead, with the unenviable task of making sure that the Kru-men and their loads got into camp in time to set up the bivouac and transport essential supplies of food and water. (At one stage, Selim was sent back with some of the men to bring up fresh supplies from Victoria.) On several occasions Selim, to Burton's relief, brought in the overloaded 'laggards'; Burton frequently refers to him as 'the excellent Selim' or 'as usual to the fore'. Selim had responsibility for measuring the various distances from Victoria with a line supplied by Lieutenant Dolben of HMS *Bloodhound*.[4]

A potentially hazardous incident occurred early on in the expedition. A chief named Botani, arrayed in an old-fashioned Royal Marine tunic of scarlet with yellow piping, and topped by a tall black hat, had performed, according to Saker, 'a lively dance, apparently borrowed from the movements of excited poultry', no doubt fuelled by the rum that had been given as a present.[5] However when Burton refused the offer of his twelve-year-old daughter, the chief went into paroxysms of rage at this insult to his 'hospitality', and it was only when Burton's party displayed their firearms as a warning that an affray was averted.[6] On his return to Victoria, Saker was challenged by local tribesmen, whereupon his men fled ahead to report his death, which was proven to be untrue when he turned up, a little late but unharmed.

The range of conditions which the party encountered was extreme. From the warm, humid, lowland forests to the bitter cold of the windy peaks, in between they were tested by the torrid heat on the great lava flows and a real shortage of water. Burton records: 'Although our botanist had despaired of finding anything potable in the absence of succulent plants, Selim Aga, wiser by experience, squeezed from the moss half a gallon of dew, sufficient to boil water for the boys during the night.'[7] In his article for the Royal Geographical Society, he attributes the saving of several lives to Selim.

After the base camp was set up at an altitude of 7,300 feet, some preliminary sorties were made: 'We assumed the right, concessible only in no-man's land, of christening the several peaks: the loftiest was honoured with the name of our Most Gracious Sovereign, and, from the highest lady in the Kingdom,' says Burton. Despite having previously inveighed against this insensitive practice, Burton's naming hierarchy simply mirrored Victorian society's obsession with ranks and titles. The highest twin peaks were named after Victoria and Albert, the party being unaware that the Prince Consort had died two days previously and that Britain was in deep mourning. Mount Helen was named after Saker's wife (who had provided their Christmas pudding), while Burton called another 'Mount Isabel', 'with similar marital dutifulness' – hardly a ringing endorsement – but 'the ceremony was concluded with a seemly libation.' Burton was also to name a smaller eminence 'Mount Selim' while Mann, in similar style, honoured his mentor, Sir William Hooker, the Director of Kew Gardens.[8]

Following an arduous sortie over the lava fields, Burton was unable to walk for a whole month and was laid up with infected lacerations to his feet. Selim 'sallied forth with Black Beggar, the cook, in search of small beasts and birds'[9] and Burton records that, apart from a previously mentioned field rat, no fewer than three animals new to science were secured. Calvo and Mann made an attempt on a mountain, but returned early when Mann fell ill with dysentery (Burton waspishly ascribes this to his teetotal habits). He himself caught up with writing his reports on the Niger and the Brass for the Foreign Office, recounting an incident in which how Selim got an unexpected ducking:

> I was compelled to seize a freighted canoe in consequence of my servant – Selim Agha, employed in the Niger Expedition of 1857 – having been thrown overboard after paying hire, by the two slaves who had charge of it, and after confiscating 24 cloths which were placed on board the *Bloodhound*.[10]

The wording suggests that this is the first mention of Selim in an official report; it also confirms that Selim actually travelled with the 1857 Niger expedition.

On 27 January, Burton with Selim and several Kru-men made their own assault on the mountain, braving freezing temperatures in their crater camp at over 10,000 feet, to reach the summit on the following day. Burton describes the scene:

> Having thus reached our goal, Selim hoisted on the very lip of the volcanic lion the Union Jack and our last bottle of champagne was emptied in honour of the day; we left a strip of lead upon which our names were roughly cut, and two sixpences in an empty bottle.[11]

On the journey back to Victoria, Selim is credited with a ruse to get the Kru-men to continue. They had been showing signs of acute exhaustion and lameness after their exertions and, by way of experiment, Selim remarked in their hearing that those who were lame might stay behind till they were well, while the others returned to 'Nanny Po'. The effect was magical. 'Every back straightened... there was a forgotten elasticity of gait and movement... we laughed at them and *with* them about their rascality.'[12] On the descent, the party was threatened by tribesmen with their eyes on plunder, and both Burton and Selim continued with revolvers cocked at the ready.[13]

If Burton needed any convincing, this first challenging expedition proved Selim to be a thoroughly reliable individual with a range of practical skills derived from his considerable experience of African travel. Quite apart from his efficiency in attending to Burton's personal wants as his steward, he had the leadership qualities and authority to keep discipline and order among the porters and guides; he was a veritable 'major domo' who ensured that things got done, and was physically tough and capable of adapting to a wide variety of situations, including surviving and acting intelligently under extremes of climate and terrain. Burton was the hardest of taskmasters and consequently his commendation speaks volumes. His later journeys in West Africa would do nothing to diminish his admiration for 'the excellent Selim'.

CHAPTER TWELVE

'Selim behaved like a trump'

From Ethiopia's utmost land;
From Zaara's fickle wilderness of sand;
From Congo's blazing plains and blooming woods...

VICTORIANS WERE FASCINATED by tales of gorillas and their apparent likeness to humans, but were quite incredulous when the French explorer Paul du Chaillu, perhaps the first European to encounter the beast, gave a graphic description of a lowland specimen in 1861, with emphasis on its ferocity. Burton was a friend of du Chaillu and backed his account, to the extent that he determined to find out the truth for himself, perhaps another example of his eternal quest for the exotic. (At this time, Europeans had not heard of the considerably larger mountain gorilla, now confined to the Virungu Mountains on the Rwanda-Congo border.) On 17 March 1862 Burton set off on the steamship HMSS *Griffon* for the Gabon River, where sightings of gorillas had been reported. Here he was in French territory, and in his record of the journey Burton describes the French settlements, the horror of the officials at the prospect of tropical disease and the competition between the French and the dominant traders. He gives an entertaining account of a dinner at a hotel at Fort Aumale, where the *table d'hôte* was under the command of a formidable French *madame*. The occasion attracted most of the French, if not the English community, who, after pre-dinner drinks on the veranda, were called to the table:

> The clientele rushed in like backwoodsmen on board a Mississippi floating palace, stripped off their coats, tucked up their sleeves, and knife in one hand and bread in the other, advanced gallantly to the fray... The din, the heat, the flare of composition candles which gave 45 per cent less of light than they ought, the blunders of the slaves, the objurgations of the hostess and the spectacled face opposite me were as much as I could bear, and a trifle more.

A quarrel as to who should carve resulted in Madame, at the head of the table, asking Selim to do the honours – an interesting reflection on his status in this company.[1] Burton also gives a vivid description of a dangerous storm as his party were on the river in a local craft powered only by oars:

> flashes of the broadest sheets inclosing fork and chain lightning... a cold blast of smelling rain, and a few drops or rather splashes, big as gooseberries and striking with a blow, are followed by a howling squall, sharp and sudden puffs... the storm sweeps the boat before it at full speed as though it had been a bit of straw. Selim and I sat with a large mackintosh sheet over our hunched backs, thus offering a breakwater to the waves.[2]

Some weeks later, a similar electrical storm almost ended their lives: Selim and Burton were huddled together, trying to light a match when:

> a sheet of white fire seemed to be let down from the black sky, passing between us with a simultaneous thundering crash and rattle, and a sulphurous smell, as if a battery had been discharged. I saw my factotum struck down whilst in the act of staggering and falling myself, we lay still for a few moments, when a mutual enquiry showed that we were both alive, only a little shaken and stunned.[3]

These incidents, among many others, indicate that Burton and Selim shared many challenging experiences in very close proximity, suggesting that, however different their cultures, a strong bond of comradeship would have formed between them.

Burton's purpose was to shoot a gorilla and if possible to buy or catch a young gorilla alive. Given the limited time at his disposal, he was not sanguine about success. He arranged a hunt, offering five dollars for any specimen shot and ten for any captured alive. Selim was 'indefatigable in his zeal', and when they heard a gorilla grunt, he pursued it with determination, but ended with no gorilla and up to his thighs in mud. (Selim did in fact shoot a fine specimen of *Sirius eboryvorus*, a squirrel, over two feet in length, which was subsequently stolen by the Kru-men.)[4] When they had almost given up and were on the return journey, local huntsmen brought Burton a dead gorilla. 'When placed in an armchair, he ludicrously suggested a pot-bellied and patriarchal negro, considerably the worse for liquor,' recounts Burton in his usual insensitive way, before giving the dimensions to prove that it was a fine specimen.[5] Selim was given the task of skinning the gorilla, and sat up half the night doing this. Unfortunately, a number of mistakes were made in the treatment of the corpse, which rapidly deteriorated in the equatorial climate. The skull, brain and sexual organs were pickled in a jar of trade rum, which was not changed for seven days, with predictable consequences. When Burton later visited his prize at the British Museum: 'The colour had changed, and the broad-chested, square-framed, pot bellied, and portly old bully boy of the woods had become a wretched pigeon-breasted, lean-flanked, shrunk-limbed, hungry-looking beggar.'[6]

On 1 August 1862 Selim was on board HMSS *Bloodhound* with Burton, bound for the ill-famed cities of Wari and Benin. Burton had found an 'official' reason for paying a visit to an area renowned for its human sacrifices and cannibalism. There had been trouble in the previous year, with reports of piracy and murder, and on 24 May there was a massed attack on the factory of a Dr Henry, who was absent at the time, but his wife was forced to flee and the factory was plundered – Mrs Henry's death a month later was attributed to the shock of this incident.[7] The British Consul from Fernando Po was obliged to seek some form of redress, and Burton saw an opportunity to investigate the customs of this notorious district. For Selim, among his many experiences in Africa, this would prove to be one of the most horrifying. Burton vividly describes the Idyare, the first coastal chief they encountered, whose 'head was surrounded by a fillet of small red bags, leopard's teeth and claws', and who apparently put his starved slaves to death without mercy and had been guilty of killing his own brother to safeguard his position.[8] This state of constant lawlessness was not helped by corrupt white traders who favoured particular chiefs and ensured their loyalty by gifts of arms, liquor, etc.

While waiting for a reply to his request to the Lagos Government for a man-of-war, Burton took the opportunity to visit Wari, about 100 miles away, leaving *Bloodhound* on a small gig, with Dr Henry and a Scots agent identified only as Captain Z. On the trip through the gloomy mangrove swamps, Burton records plentiful wildlife, including cranes, kingfishers, fish-hawks, sharks, crocodiles and the equally ferocious mangrove flies.

Wari had been the site of a Portuguese mission since the 1680s but was now in a decrepit, corrupt state. Justice was not known there: the poison ordeal was practised as a means of determining the guilt or innocence of an accused person. Wealthier locals mixed cast-off European apparel with local styles, and Burton comments scathingly that frock coats, tile hats and gaudy umbrellas did not go well with prominent cicatrices between scalp and nose, or huge wrist and ankle rings of brass, pewter, or coral.[9] He was equally contemptuous of the chiefs' lifestyle:

1. Andrew Thurburn, with the family copy of *Incidents from the Life of Selim Aga*. Behind him is a portrait of his great, great grandfather Robert Thurburn, in consular uniform.

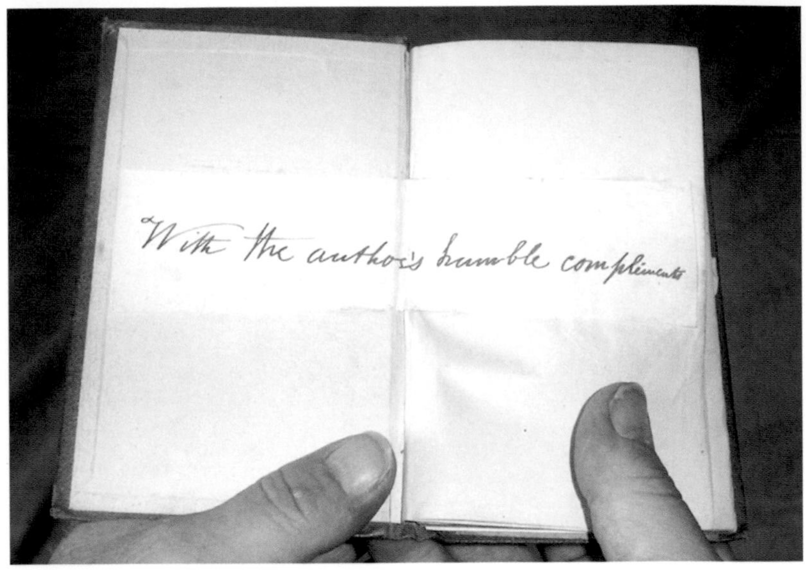

2. The author's inscription on Andrew Thurburn's copy of *Incidents from the Life of Selim Aga*

3. Caravan crossing dunes (*Shadows Across the Sahara*, John Hare, 2001)

4. Nuba village scene (George Rodger Estate)

5. Young Nuba goat herders (George Rodger Estate)

6. Slave market at Cairo

7. Interview with the Viceroy of Egypt at his palace in Alexandria
(Plates 6, 7 and 8 are from paintings by David Roberts and are reproduced courtesy of George D Lintzeris, Petra Fine Arts)

8. Slave boat on the Nile

9. Deeside view
(Photograph: James McCarthy)

10. *The Visit of the Patron and Patroness to the Village School* (detail)
Thomas Faed (McManus Galleries, Dundee City Council Leisure and Arts)

11. Murtle House (Photograph: James McCarthy)

12. The display of the King Gelele's wealth. From *Dahomey and the Dahomans* (1851) by F Forbes (as is plate below).

13. The Atto or Platform Customs

14. Richard Burton in disguise for his journey to Mecca
From *The Life of Captain Sir Richard Burton* (1898) by Lady Isabel Burton
(Plates 12, 13 and 14 are reproduced courtesy of the Trustees of the National Library of Scotland)

> The life of a 'native gentleman' in these rivers consists of rising with the sun, drinking, snuffing and smoking till 10 o'clock breakfast, a heavy siesta, and an honest debauch for the rest of the day, interrupted only by supper after sunset.

He makes the point, however, that the local whites did likewise.[10]

En route to Benin, Burton was sufficiently incensed by the thieving of his Kru-men to report that most of one day was passed in flogging them, one receiving four dozen lashes. He reports that he had never yet managed to drink his last bottle of cognac – as it had always been stolen. No doubt this occurred when porters lagged behind (deliberately, in Burton's opinion) and Selim, as before, was delegated to bring up the main body of Kru-men with the baggage. The party by this time consisted of no less than fifty-one, including the four whites. They were plagued by lack of water, and on one occasion were forced to go to bed supperless after a nine-hour march.[11]

On the following day their tempers were not improved when they reached the outskirts of Benin to find the city guarded by a 'Captain of War', who was so weighed down with ornaments that his attendants had to support his arms. Already drunk and with his face smeared with blood from a recent goat sacrifice, this individual addressed them rudely and then attempted to steal a chain and seal. Further on, they passed a recently crucified man. Burton was horrified to learn that this crucifixion had been done in honour of his visit – although he was not sufficiently horrified to desist from sketching the scene. On the following morning, just outside the door of his hut, he found yet another murdered slave, no doubt a further token of the king's respect for his honoured guest.[12] What Selim thought of this is not recorded.

Benin was a veritable Golgotha; according to Burton, the

king 'removes heads with exemplary insouciance... at times the streets of the capital run red with blood'. The city stank of death, with mildewed skulls along the way, 'lying around like pebbles'. Alongside the highways leading to the palace were buzzard-infested graveyards.[13] The main square, overlooked by Burton's hut, was littered with human bones. He describes the ghastly sight of a young woman raised on a stool about ten feet above the ground with her eyes pecked out, a sacrifice to the 'rain fetish'.[14]

Burton forwarded a number of showy presents to the king, as was the custom, but was angered by the inordinate delay in meeting with the court and the lack of food: it was usual for such a visiting party to be fed. Eventually, Burton and the ship's commander, decked out in full uniform and cocked hats, were received, attended by Selim and two Kru-men dressed in white pants, blue frock coats and armed with cutlasses.[15] The impressive king was attended by a large crowd of courtiers and naked 'cutlass boys', but again Burton was made furious by the king's deliberate withholding of permission to leave the city. One way and another the travellers were subjected to bad behaviour and pilfering by anyone who could lay their hands on their goods.

On their way out of Benin, Selim collected half a dozen skulls, but since such objects were 'fetish' or witchcraft objects, the porters refused to carry them, and so he had to shoulder this load himself. When the Kru-men asked what he wanted with these gruesome relics, Burton teasingly replied that, 'the poor feller, who could get no sustenance from yours, wished to grind these bones and make his bread'.[16] Selim would have been much amused by this sally. The skulls were forwarded to a Dr Davis, who ascertained they had belonged to young women, who had presumably been sacrificed.

The last reference to Selim on this journey is when he found a young boy, suspected of previous theft, with one of Burton's shirts fastened to his load. The boy, frightened out of his wits, took to his heels and narrowly escaped being shot – whether by Selim or another is not recorded.[17] It was with a feeling of a great load of wickedness being lifted from their shoulders that they eventually reached the *Bloodhound* and returned to the comparative civilisation of Fernando Po.

On 22 August 1863 Selim started out on a journey up the mighty Congo. At the end of this exploration, he would have the unusual distinction of having travelled along the three greatest rivers on the continent: the Congo, the Nile and the Niger. Burton records that, 'the party consisted of the Commander, Mr Bigley and five chosen "Griffons", including William Deane, boatswain's mate, as good a man as his namesake in Blake's day', and 'the estimable Friend, captain's cook and Figaro in general' – a reference to Selim.[18] Mention has already been made to the mystery surrounding the authorship of 'A Trip Up the Congo', which appeared in the *Geographical Magazine* of July 1875 and, except where attributed to Burton's narrative of 1876, the quotes below are from that source.

The journey itself was the usual woeful tale of recalcitrant porters and grasping chiefs, all of this expressed with Burton's usual bile and vituperation; Selim's account is considerably more objective. Burton devotes a whole chapter to his views regarding slavery and missions in this region, but apart from some casual specimen collecting, the 'trip' was exactly that, to satisfy Burton's wish to view the Congo cataracts. The opening remarks of Selim's article are somewhat surprising:

> Before starting on an exploratory journey into any part of Africa, it is essential that the traveller should be properly

> equipped and provided with the necessary kit both for the inward and outward man; clothing, blankets, and waterproofs of every description; tea, coffee, and sugar if the latter is desirable; a few bottles of genuine cognac, or some 10-year-old Jamaica rum.[19]

While the slightly didactic wording is characteristic of Selim, the need for high quality alcohol comes straight from Burton, who was a great believer in its efficacy in warding off tropical disease. Selim describes a relatively uneventful journey up the first stretch of the river.

On Saturday 5 September they 'arrived at King Nesalla's village, and having settled an altercation with the canoe men, who wanted more pay... made a fresh start.' There follows an encounter with the chief at Embomma, who 'came to levy contributions from us. His people, who were armed with guns and matchlocks, made various warlike gestures, and ordered us to stop... we were compelled to pay one bottle of rum, and a piece of cloth twelve fathoms in length.' At one point, Selim was instructed to keep guard while the chief inspected all of the party's goods.

A tough march up hill and down dale into the interior elicits the adjective 'irksome' from Selim; Burton describes the descent as a '*malevoie*, over slabs and boulders, loose stones and clayey ground, slippery as ice after rain. The moleques [slaves] descended like chamois within twenty minutes: Selim and I with booted feet, took double the time.' The party then met with the king of Kaye:

> We found him seated in state, dressed up in motley garb of European manufacture, a white shirt with collar turned down, a crimson velvet loin cloth fringed with gold, tied

> round the waist by means of a belt, the handle of which was made of nickel silver, being very showily ornamented with imitation emeralds and ruby garnets. Over all his dress was a beadle's red cloak, and on his head a helmet resembling those worn by English Life Guardsmen.[20]

Interestingly, the wording of this description of the king is identical in both accounts. The king, Sudikil, was apparently dissatisfied with the gifts presented by the party and refused to provide food for them. Eventually an agreement was reached with Sudukil and his father, Gidi Mavunga, to retain all the party's travelling gear in return for providing food and accompanying Burton and his men up the Congo to Yellala, and from there to St Salvador. Other local personages tried to get in on the act: Prince Nelonga demanded the same presents as had been given to Sudikil, which was refused. At this point, Selim amused himself by carving Burton's initial in a large baobab tree while 'my master arranges some botanical specimens'. Selim does not mention his part in this work, but Burton's narrative states: 'with Factotum Selim's assistance, I managed to collect some 490 specimens within the fortnight'.[21] These specimens were forwarded to Kew Gardens for identification and are listed in an appendix to Burton's published account.

The cunning Gidi Mavunga attempted to distract Burton by seduction, allowing village women to enter his quarters unescorted. Burton, who was not immune to the beauty of African women, whom he sometimes describes in great physiognomic detail and occasionally sketches, recognised this as an old trick. To succumb would have led to the confiscation of all his goods, or worse. 'Foiled in his benevolent attempt, the covetous senior presently entered the hut, and began unceremoniously to open a package of cloth which did not belong to him. Selim cocked his revolver, and placed it handy, so the goods were afterwards respected,' says Burton.[22]

Later, when they attempted to leave the village of Vivi, Chief Nesalla came with over 100 armed men, attempting with this show of strength to stop the party proceeding to Yellala. In his account Burton simply refers the reader to Selim's narrative:

> Five or six persons spoke, and the conference lasted an hour. The result was that the cloth we had with us was not enough, and the princes of Yellala must get a different piece from that which was before the conference, and no division into two pieces was to be made of it under any consideration whatsoever. As the whole affair was conducted in a good-humoured manner my master agreed to the terms. In the evening the inhabitants of the village had a dance, which ended in drunkenness and uproar.[23]

To secure the services of the guides and porters beyond Yellala, Burton proposed sending for more cloth, powder and rum, albeit half of what was demanded. Gidi Mavunga, 'quite beyond self-control, sprang up and declared that if the Mundele would not follow him, that obstinate person might remain behind... he rushed off and disappeared in the bush, followed by part of his slaves.' During this incident, Burton claims that 'Selim behaved like a trump,' but does not elaborate.[24]

In fact, the expedition got no further than the first, not overly impressive, cataracts at Yellala. The cost in trade goods of proceeding further was deemed prohibitive: the equivalent of £300 in cloth, liquor and beads for a three-day march. The return to the mouth of the Congo was made even more hazardous by drunken canoemen. At one stage, only a show of arms prevented piracy, with the canoemen forced to proceed at gunpoint. All in all, this expedition, which lasted approximately five weeks, seems to have been particularly fraught and in the end there was little other than the botanical collection to show for it.

CHAPTER THIRTEEN
Two Thousand ‘Amazons’

In these romantic regions Man grows wild;
Here dwells the Negro, nature's outcast child,
Scorned by his brethren.

THE LAST JOURNEY that Selim made as Burton's servant proved to be the longest, and perhaps the strangest. On 29 November 1863, he departed with the rest of the party on HMSS *Antelope* on an expedition to the Kingdom of Dahome, where King Gelele had a reputation for slave trading and indulging in ceremonial human sacrifices. Burton's commission was to try to persuade Gelele to stop the former and at least not to conduct the latter in the presence of visitors such as the official consul. He was also asked to ascertain the fate of some Christian prisoners and to secure their release. Burton had been to Dahome previously, almost certainly without official blessing, and impressed the king by keeping his promise to return. Personally, Burton was fascinated by the prospect of finding out more about the human sacrifices, and, above all, of reporting on Gelele's legendary army of women soldiers, the 'Amazons'; on his previous visit, Burton had been made an honorary commander of a company of these female warriors. The 'persuasion' of the king was to be aided by a collection of gaudy presents; unfortunately these did not include the carriage and horses which Gelele expected.

The party of almost 100 started out from Whydah [Ouidah] on 5 December. *En route* they passed through an empty landscape where warfare had clearly taken its toll. As they drew closer to Gelele's country seat at Kana, elaborate ceremonial welcomes by the king's messengers were an unwelcome impediment to progress. When they eventually reached Kana, Burton was impressed by Gelele's appearance – he was a tall, athletic and broad shouldered young man – but less so by the mere nine-gun salute which he received, and he imperiously insisted on the eleven-gun performance granted Commodore Frederick Forbes, who had visited Gelele ten years earlier.[1] Forbes had been given the present of a little slave girl previously destined to be sacrificed on the king's tomb, her own parents having been decapitated. In a repetition of Selim's experience and at much the same age, Sarah Forbes Bonetta, as she was subsequently christened, was brought back to England for her education. She became fluent in English, was accomplished in music, and, according to Forbes, 'won the affections of all who have known her... her head is considered so excellent a phrenological specimen, and illustrating such high intellect, that Mr Pistrucci, the medallist of the mint, has undertaken to take a bust of her.'

Burton was unimpressed by the armed 'Amazons', who numbered about a quarter of what he had been led to expect. He declared them all to be ugly, although this was possibly only to reassure his wife Isabel, for whom he drew a sketch to prove his point. But he also notes this in a private letter to a friend:

> I looked forward to seeing 5,000 African Virgins with the liveliest curiosity, having never in my life seen a Negress in such predicament. Imagine my disappointment at finding them to be chiefly wives taken in adultery and given to the king for soldiering instead of being killed. They are mostly old and fearfully ugly... Selim my factotum carefully counted them all and made them amount to 2,038.[2]

The royal procession may have made up for this. It was accompanied by drums, horns, the firing of muskets and preceded by droves of dignitaries, relatives and fetish men. Gelele was guarded by 500 musketeers, and followed by innumerable slaves bearing boxes of valuables. The women soldiers paraded, singing, dancing and firing off their muskets; some carried platters of human skulls, no doubt of enemy tribesmen. The king was borne in a hammock of yellow silk, surmounted by brightly coloured

The chief of the 'Amazons', sketched by Burton
(Trustees of the National Library of Scotland)

parasols. The din was indescribable and, not surprisingly, Burton retired early with a headache.

The presentation of the British government's gifts was something of a disaster. The crimson tent, derided by the king as too small, collapsed when Burton's party attempted to erect it, while the silver belts were no substitute for the bracelets which Gelele wanted. The coat of mail was too heavy and the gauntlets were too small. Above all, the carriage and white horses which Gelele had previously requested were missing, and Burton had a difficult task explaining why these had not been provided. Gelele announced it was not a propitious time to deliver the government's message, and delayed an official audience for this purpose for several weeks. During this irritating hiatus, Burton was given ample evidence of the annual 'customs' involving human sacrifice, which he had timed his visit to observe – if not the executions themselves. He and Selim were revolted by the sight of skulls nailed up around the palace, and they saw a prisoner awaiting decapitation, his mouth kept open by a forked stick.

Burton was given permission to visit the victims' shed with Gelele, after which he secured a pardon for some of the prisoners. But after the 'Evil Night', when he heard the decapitations being carried out, he witnessed several corpses propped up on stools, and others hung by their heels. The 'Amazons' conducted their own executions of probably around forty women. Burton reckoned that the total number killed, of both sexes, over several days of 'festivities', was about eighty – far fewer than had been expected based on previous reports. What he did not see was the bizarre Atto or 'Platform Customs', when the victims, sitting on boat-shaped platforms were propelled over a wall to be beheaded below, as described previously by the horrified Commander Forbes.

During these 'customs', the king performed a marathon dance, with Burton and members of his party obliged to join in; at one point, Burton excelled himself by dancing solo in front of his own company of 'Amazons', to their great approbation and that of the crowd. Selim was not invited to join Burton and Gelele in drinking trade rum from the skulls of enemy chiefs mounted in brass. What Selim made of all this is not recorded. Despite the apparent conviviality, Gelele rejected all of Burton's requests regarding slavery, and claimed that the Christian prisoners he was supposed to have, were dead. He was in no mood to modify his customs, although he had ensured that Burton did not actually witness the executions, probably to the latter's disappointment.

By the time Burton reached Whydah on 18 February, after the 'most comfortless' march he had endured in Africa, his party had been on expedition for over two and a half months. He indented for the sum of £128.10s.3d. for all expenses, including sixty bags of cowrie shells. The Foreign Office, no doubt mindful of his waywardness, reminded him that any publication related to the trip would have to be perused by Lord Walpole in the first instance, and his decision would determine what could be seen by the public.[3]

On 7 May 1864, Burton left Fernando Po and his trusted and greatly valued factotum for good. After almost three years of extraordinary experiences and adventures together, it would have been an emotional leave-taking for both. There appears to be no other record of Selim's activities from this point until his death in 1875. According to Burton writing after he left Fernando Po, Selim had resolved to travel to the source of the Niger. The last letter Burton received from him was sent from Liberia.

CHAPTER FOURTEEN
The Last Adventure

Let Britain's sons the fruitful coast explore,
And kindly bless the race they wrong'd before;
With gentle promises invite to toil,
With precious gifts endow the docile soil;
Till Afric's race in grateful rev'rence bend,
And hail the teacher where they find the friend.

AS OFTEN ELSEWHERE in his life, there is a mystery surrounding Selim's last years. Farwell, one of Burton's most rigorous biographers, states that Selim was killed in Liberia during the Grebo War, but without giving a source for this. There was internal turmoil in Liberia almost from the inception of the colony in the late 1840s, ironically between emancipated slaves from the USA and indigenous African tribes. From the beginning of the nineteenth century, concern was being expressed among the leaders of society in the United States about the numbers of freed slaves. The successful Haitian insurrection led by Dominique Toussaint l'Ouverture triggered anxiety that a race war might be ignited if this revolt was exported to the American slave states; many, even in the northern states, did not believe that ex-slaves could be tolerated in a predominantly white society. Thus a policy of returning slaves 'back to the land of their fathers' became the object of the American Colonisation Society, founded in 1816. Britain had established a similar colony in Sierra Leone in 1787 for the same purpose, to deal with a much smaller number – about 1,500 – after the 1772 legal manumission of all slaves in Britain.

From its beginnings, the American Colonisation Society was in an informal partnership with the US government, whose Presidents, from Monroe onwards, supported this resettlement project, with Liberia selected as the most suitable location. Unsurprisingly, many former slaves saw Liberia as a 'dumping ground' and the policy of colonisation as the enemy of abolition. There was no suggestion at this time that slavery was to be abolished in the southern slave states of America. Forcible deportation would be resorted to if voluntary colonisation was not effective. At the same time, the slave trade was to be stopped, primarily to halt the influx of Africans into the USA – although in practice, in the first half of the century, more than a million slaves were transported to the slave states.

The first colonist ship from America, the *Elizabeth*, set sail in January 1820 carrying eighty-six men, women and children. They were bound for the notoriously unhealthy coastlands of West Africa and after many deaths and difficulties, they retreated to Freetown in Sierra Leone. Despite this setback, separate settlements from different American states were established along the coast over the next twenty years and in 1847, Liberia became an independent republic. Although the initial settlement at Cape Mesurado had been reluctantly negotiated by treaty, conflict between the settlers and the native peoples developed almost from the beginning of colonisation, notably with the Kru and Grebo-speaking populations. Ironically, this was primarily because the incoming colonists, notwithstanding their own history, regarded the aboriginal Africans as inferior, while the colonists exploited differences between the native clans for their own purposes. The indigenous Africans were excluded from citizenship, under a government entirely controlled by the settlers, unless they adopted the manners and lifestyle of western 'civilised society'.

There were several other sources of discontent. At a time of great economic hardship for the colonists, they attempted to control traditional Grebo and Kru coastal trade through the ports. There were also disputes over land, especially around Cape Palmas, and jurisdiction over the interior. Maryland County in the south had founded an Episcopal college for local Africans, who were then accused by the settlers of getting ideas above their station and challenging the state. After the first Grebo War of 1856–57, when the Grebos were defeated, Maryland formally united with Liberia.

On 31 December 1873, Grebo leaders representing various tribal factions proclaimed the 'Grebo Reunited Kingdom or Confederation'. They asked for assistance from the British governors of Sierra Leone and Cape Coast for protection, but talks with American Liberians failed and hostilities began in September 1875. Grebos from the Grand Cess District attempted to drive out the entire Liberian colony after a dispute over land which the Liberians of Monrovia claimed had been ceded to the colony of Maryland. The Grebo inflicted a series of crushing defeats on the Liberian militia and American intervention was called for. Only the dispatch of the USS *Alaska* by President Ulysses S Grant ended the insurrection, and in 1876 a treaty was signed disbanding the Grebo Confederation.

Although Selim's death in this conflict, repeated in several biographies of Burton, has not been verified, there is no reason to doubt its veracity. How he became involved is unknown. Nor is there any indication of whether he died as a combatant or simply as an incidental casualty of war. If the former, it is intriguing to conjecture where his allegiance might have lain. Given his views on slavery and the altruism exemplified by his proposals for the amelioration of Africa, it would not be surprising if he had sided with the native people, who were undoubtedly discriminated against and who had just cause to oppose their arrogant enemies. But that is mere speculation. Lady Glover, in her biography of her husband, says, 'It is believed that... [Selim] was at length killed while attending to the wounded after a tribal battle somewhere in Liberia.'[1] If true, it would be fitting that an adventurous and heroic life ended heroically.

EPILOGUE

Do what thy manhood bids thee do, from
None but self expect applause;
He noblest lives and noblest dies who makes
And keeps his self-made laws.

All other life is living death, a world where
None but phantoms dwell,
A breath, a wind, a sound, a voice, a tinkling
Of the camel bell.
...
Wend now thy way with brow serene, fear
Not thy humble tale to tell:
The whispers of the Desert-wind; the tinkling
of the camel's bell.

from 'The Kasidah of Haji Abdu El-Yezdi'
Richard Burton

SELIM'S LIAISON WITH a local woman while he was at Murtle resulted in the birth of a son on 6 August 1847, christened Alexander Aga. (Unusually, the birth certificate refers to him as 'illegitimate'.) The name of the mother is given as Jane Hunter, while Selim is registered as a domestic servant. There were a number of women named Jane Hunter in the vicinity of Murtle at that time; she might have been the sister of a local farmer of that name, and at thirty-three, was considerably older than Selim. Whatever the circumstances, this birth must have caused considerable local comment, although illegitimacy in rural Aberdeenshire was twice the national average, accounting for one in five births.

Alexander Aga himself had a family; on the birth certificate of Mary Jane Aga in 1873 in Aberdeen he is registered as a 'boot-closer', ie someone who stitches together the different parts of the boot or shoe. There is a continuous family line in Scotland down to the present day.

In Selim's known writings, there is no mention of his son or of visiting his Scottish family. The most obvious reason for this might be that his early autobiography may have been composed before the birth of Alexander, while the second text, his plan for Africa, would have been an inappropriate context for any reference to this family. It is also just possible that Jane Hunter had left the district early in her pregnancy and that Selim was unaware of the birth of his son.

A fascinating and quite unexpected development from my research on Selim Aga's life has been the discovery via the internet of direct descendants living in Scotland and the USA, and also those of Robert Thurburn. As a result of a short request for information placed on a genealogical website in 2003, I was contacted by Marion Walls of Kirkintilloch, intimating that she was the great-great-great-granddaughter of Selim. Her own

Anno Domini 1847

July 20.

Hutcheon — James Hutcheon & Jane Low Findon had twins born 9th ult. & baptized Mary & Anne. Wit: J. M. Donald & Thos Hutcheon

.24.

Walker — Robert Walker & Elizabeth Bartlett Portlethen had a daughter born 9th ult. & baptized Elizabeth Duguid. Wit: J. R. Davidson Esqr & P. Duguid Esqr of Auchlunies

.31.

Stewart — John Stewart & Anne Wright Badentoy had a son born 11th ult. & baptized William. A. Paterson & Jas Robbie

.31.

Main — John Main & Margaret Craig Portlethen had a son born 24th ult. and baptized William. Wit: Jas Craig & Robt Main

August 6.

Knowles — George Knowles & Jane Wood Downies had a son born 20th ult. & baptized George. Wit: Christian & Jas Wood.

.21.

Masson — James Masson & Helen Robb Portlethen had a daughter born 30th ult. & baptized Elizabeth. Wit: Geo: & Eliz: Masson.

Sept. 11.

Wood — Moses Wood & Elspet Knowles Downies had a son born 29th ult. & baptized James. Wit: Geo: Knowles & Moses Wood.

.18.

Wood — John Wood & Anne Craig Portlethen had a daughter born 11th ult. & baptized Betty. Wit: Geo Wood & Jas Craig

.27.

Aga — Selim Aga, Muirtle, & Jane Hunter, Aberdeen had an illegitimate son born 6th August & baptized Alexander

.30.

Extract from the record of the birth of Selim's son, Alexander Hunter Aga (reproduced with the kind permission of the Registrar General for Scotland)

genealogical enquiries, supported by official parish records, show that she is indeed a direct descendant, and I am especially grateful to her for her work in that respect. I was later contacted by Lynn Adams of Cumbernauld near Glasgow, whose mother's maiden name was Aga and whose grandmother was the daughter of Alexander Hunter Aga, Selim's son.

Meanwhile, I had heard from Don Crevie of Seattle (whom I had the pleasure of meeting on his visit to Scotland in 2004) that he was the great-great-grandson of Selim, the other Crevies of that generation in the USA being his brother David and cousin Karen. The Crevie surname came from an ancestor who had emigrated to USA in the nineteenth century, coincidentally from Aberdeen.

On the Thurburn side, I was particularly pleased to make contact with Robert Thurburn's great-great-grandson, Andrew Thurburn of London, who kindly showed me Robert Thurburn's portrait and his consular swords and very helpfully provided the results of his father's research on the family, including a number of important references to Robert's time in Alexandria.

In recent years interest in black people brought to Scotland has increased considerably with articles in the press and radio programmes on this topic – although none of these have referred to Selim. Almost all refer to the Atlantic slave trade, with its connections to West Africa and the Americas. James Robertson's prize-winning novel *Joseph Knight*, based on the true story of a slave brought back from the West Indies to Scotland somewhat earlier than Selim, has been widely acclaimed. I have published short articles on Selim in *Scottish Book Collector* and in the magazine of the Black and Asian Studies Association; material has also been provided for publication in Arabic on the Sudanonline website at the request of Yassir Abidi Beredewil, a Sudanese who has taken a continuing interest in what appears to be the only written record of its kind for this period in the history of the Sudan.

At the time of writing, the Sudan is receiving considerable media coverage as a result of the depredations of Arab militia on the farming populations of Darfur, which has in many ways an uncanny and chilling similarity to the situation which obtained in Kordofan in the first half of the nineteenth century. Although Selim, in one of his publications, refers to himself as being a native of Darfur, Taqali is now accepted as being in the province of Kordofan to the east of Darfur. There is a certain irony that another tragedy was unfolding in Liberia: the United States sent a warship in 2003 to support the government there in its offensive against local militias, in many ways a replica of the war 130 years ago in which Selim apparently lost his life, and in which the US took similar action.

The first half of the nineteenth century was a time of intense activity on the part of those who fought for the abolition of slavery, inevitably in the teeth of opposition from entrenched commercial interests. A signal victory was won in the passing of the Foreign Slave Trade Act in 1807, albeit that this was intended primarily to pre-empt the slaving activities of France and Spain. This Act effectively prohibited the use of British ports and shipping, which had dominated this trade, from being used for the transport of slaves. Almost simultaneously, the USA passed a similar Act. Equally, if not more important, the abolition of the slave trade throughout the British empire in 1838, some two years after Selim's arrival in Scotland, is estimated to have freed some 800,000 men, women and children. However, apart from the difficulty of actually implementing these enactments, they did not by any means extinguish slavery *per se*. Further, since they were targeted on the Atlantic trade, mainly between West Africa and the Americas, they had little effect on Islamic slavery. The fact that slaves of the same age as Selim when he was captured have in recent years been sold at public auction in the Nuba Mountains, combined with the testimony of Mende Nazer described above, still represents a major humanitarian challenge in the twenty-first century.

APPENDIX 1

the full text of

Incidents Connected with the Life of Selim Aga

by Selim Aga

Dedication to Mrs Thurburn Murtle, June 1846

Madam, – Having written a short account of some incidents connected with my life, I return my grateful and sincere thanks to you for the great interest you have taken in my education, by which means I have been brought from African darkness to a knowledge of the comforts of a civilized and social life. Hitherto, for these ten years, I have experienced your benevolent care and tuition, and have been elevated far above many of my poor countrymen, whose minds are lying with the dust. To whom should I ascribe this work, if not to the patroness of my education? To whom should I dedicate these incidents, if not to the guardian of my younger years? Yes, Madam; to you, and to you alone, I now acknowledge my gratitude for the many benefits which I enjoy. Although far distant from kindred and relations – although far from the care of an overlooking mother – I have found in you, Madam, a truly good substitute for these wants. I have experienced your goodness in sending me to school, and putting me in the hands of one whose whole interest was absorbed in teaching the young idea how to shoot. In whatever circumstances my lot may be cast, I hope your private admonitions will render me impregnable when attacked by the many vices prevalent in the world.

I have the honour to be,
Madam,
Your most obedt. Servant,

Selim Aga

Preface

IT IS NOT the author's intention to make great orations out of nothing, nor to picture the description of his country in eloquent language, but to give, in the form of recollections, a brief account of incidents connected with his own life. Having been urged by several friends to write an account of his life, he hopes that this small work will meet the approbation of all who read it. He will not fail, therefore, to make it as interesting as possible. The reader, however, must not expect something extraordinary when beginning to read this narrative. Great anxiety has been felt by geographical and other societies, to obtain an accurate knowledge of Africa and its products. Of these, the author is sorry that he cannot satisfy his readers, having been taken away from his country at a very early age. Of all the quarters of the globe, Africa is the least known. Ignorance, barbarity, and superstition, prevail in its centre, and the unhealthy nature of its climate renders it almost impracticable for any European to travel into it, and satisfy an enquiring public. Taking a natural view of the country, it is barren, sandy, and mountainous, interspersed with a few green spots, called oases, or made fertile by the inundation of some river in the rainy season. Taking an artificial view of those regions, you will perceive nothing but a few small huts here and there, built by the inhabitants for their own accommodation. The Northern and Southern States can boast of a little civilization, being frequented and inhabited by the dwellers of the north temperate zone. In taking a political view of the centre of Africa, the enquirer will find the country divided into a number of small principalities, who maintain their dignity by making war against each other. The captives taken in these wars are sold as slaves, being purchased by Arabs and Turks on the east coast, and Spaniards, Portuguese, and Americans, on the west. Thus many of these poor creatures are brought to a level with the brute beasts, by the inhabitants of that federal government (the United States) who pretend to profess the principles of freedom and Christianity in their truest light. The selling of these captives stimulates others to kidnap some of the poor natives, and carry on a brutal traffic in buying and selling human victims for the gratification of their own ambitious propensities. In this manner the fate of the author was sealed. The author will proceed to detail the events of his history in the form of recollections.

Description of the Valley of Tegla and its Inhabitants

SURROUNDED BY SOME beautiful mountain scenery, and situated between Durfur and Abyssinia, is a small valley going under the denomination of Tegla, or Tegeley. To this valley I stretch forth my affections, giving it the endearing appellation of my native home and fatherland. It was there that I was born; 'twas there that I received the fond looks of a loving mother; and it was there that I set my feet for the first time upon a world full of cares, trials, difficulties, and dangers. I cannot give the exact limits of the valley of Tegla. There were, however, three Chiefs who exercised power over its inhabitants. Mehemet Chammaroo (under whose government my father was) ruled the centre; while two other princes had the sway, one on each side. Like many of the regions bordering on the equator, the valley of Tegla is exposed to the excessive heat of the burning sun. Its seasons, properly speaking, can only be divided into two parts – the rainy and the dry season. In the rainy season agriculture is carried on by the farmer on a very small scale – the only substitute for a plough being a long pole, with something similar to a shovel attached to the end of it. With this instrument the surface of the ground is broken, after which the seed (consisting of Indian corn and maize) is sown in small quantities at certain distances from each other. After it has grown a certain length, part of it is transplanted into different fields, thus giving the crop full scope and encouragement to grow. When the corn begins to change colour, the rainy season declines, till at length the refulgent rays of the sun perceive the inhabitant of the vale preparing to reap his harvest. The rain is over, the dry season is on; many begin to reap the fruits of their labour.

How wisely has Providence ordered all things. The inhabitants of Egypt have no rain, and yet the river Nile has its yearly inundations. The rainy season in the valley of Tegla, and its neighbouring countries forms tributaries to the Nile; makes it overflow its banks; spreads fertility through the muddy soil of the country; and supplies its dependant natives with the necessaries of life.

My juvenile recollections did not bring the nature of the implements used for shearing. The shearers are not formed of a number of mercenaries, who expect to pocket shillings and half-crowns at the end of their period of labour; but such is the social nature of the people among themselves, that they exchange services with each other. A large concourse of them assemble in the harvest field; and, in a very short time, the harvest is taken in. The day of shearing is generally ended with dancing, of which amusement they are very fond. The reader, perhaps, will inquire what sort of drink these dancers use? His mind will very likely answer, Jamaica rum, French brandy, or Irish whisky. But no; water is their chief drink. They have a thick intoxicating liquor, which they make from the Indian corn; but such a luxury is only used on extraordinary occasions. After all their harvest festivities are over, they give themselves up to all the indolent habits prevalent in these eastern countries; and lounge in their booths until the appearance of the skies proclaim the distant approach of the rainy season.

Widely different is the dry season, when compared with the rainy. In the dry season the inhabitant of the vale employs his time with various pursuits; building, hunting, travelling, and warfare, generally in this season. Every grown up man is a warrior.

In the rainy, nothing but agriculture occupies his attention. In the dry season he has to dig wells to supply his household with water; in the rainy, he has only to go to the rivulets for that supply. The dry season carries off all traces of water; scorches all the grass and green trees; occasions deep chasms in the earth; and leaves the poor native nothing to depend upon but his industry in the rainy season. Indian corn, maize, and a flock of goats are generally all his treasure. Money is not valued. The valley of Tegla boasts of no cows, although many are kept in its vicinity. Prince Chammaroo's dominions had only three wells. The different districts regularly awaited their turn in receiving a supply of water. The religion is Paganism, mixed with several Mahommedan rites, such as the shaving of their heads, circumcision, and fasting; but their chief attention is attracted to the sun, the moon, and stars.

About a month after the ceremony of circumcision, a number of young men convene at the house where the rite had been performed, and sally from thence through the country on hunting excursions. Everything falls a prey to the hunter's knife and spear; and on these occasions the poultry-yard suffers most, while the poor owners are mere lookers-on at these depredations, it being deemed sacred to interfere with the behaviour of these young men. Fasting is also very strictly observed by the devotee, one month in the year being allotted for that purpose. Before daybreak, he rises and eats, and never again tastes anything, until the evening stars declare the shades of night, when he breaks his fast and retires to rest. The houses in the valley of Tegla are built in a style peculiar to themselves. Every room is built about ten or twenty yards from each other, of a round form, with thatch roofs. The under part of the rooms are built of stones and mud; the roofs are thatched with the maize and Indian corn canes. Four or five rooms form a respectable dwelling, the whole of which are enclosed by a wall about five feet high, thus leaving an open square in the centre. In the great heat of the dry season, this square is used by the in-dwellers for sleeping apartments, where they all lie down on the floor, and cover themselves with a large white sheet. If disturbed by any wild beasts during the night, they betake themselves to the inner rooms. My father's house consisted of two bedrooms, a kitchen, a mill room, and a goat room, or fold. Goat's milk is considered a very wholesome commodity; it has a pleasing sweet taste, which attracts the palate to it, and is said to possess a certain virtue in medicinal qualities. The junior male members of the family are employed in taking care of the flock. When a number of them are going in the same direction they mix their flocks together, and each in his turn mutually takes care of the whole flock till evening, when, by a cry peculiar to each goat-herd, his flock separates from the rest, and follows him. He then takes them home, gets them milked, and secures them in the fold. Those which are great favourites are generally taken into the sleeping apartments. The milk must not be allowed to stand till the middle of next day, else it would get quite sour. In order to prevent this catastrophe they either drink it or make butter of it. Their mode of churning is as follows:

The gourd, or calabash, which grows plentifully in these districts, is a plant something similar to a melon plant. It's fruit is like a melon, but the inside is bitter. The gourd melons grow to different sizes, so that the natives make dishes and plates out of them, by cutting them into halves. The churn, however, requires a whole melon, and one of the largest is taken for that purpose. After a part of the pith is taken out, it is filled with water, and permitted to stand till the inside is quite rotten. It is then cleaned out, secured into a rope basket, suspended to the roof of one of the rooms, so as it can be reached by a person standing, and there it serves as a churn – the dairymaid's work being to put the milk into it, and work it to and fro with her hands. No cream is extracted.

The butter is generally used for rubbing their skins; and very little clothing being used, many of them could be seen standing out in the sun like a number of polished statues. After washing themselves with water, they never think that they are complete till they rub some butter on their skins. The dress among the higher classes is a long wide gown, reaching to the ankles, and wide open sleeves, so as not to confine the wearer too much, and sandals on their feet. The lower classes, again, have a long wide plaid, which they tie round their body, and over one of their shoulders, leaving the other quite free; while in length it only reaches to the knees. This forms all their variety of dress.

Their food is entirely confined to the Indian corn, served up in different ways. They seldom kill their goats for butcher meat, having a great desire to preserve a large stock.

Having given a short account of the customs of my native country, I shall now relate my own history.

Self-History – Youth and Premature Slavery

YOUTH IS THE period in which true happiness is enjoyed. It is the time when all trials and difficulties seem to lie in oblivion; and it is then that all principles can be instilled into the tender mind. The mind in youth is not prejudiced, builds many castles in the air although without any symptoms of ambition, is pleased and always desires to please. It is like the shoot of a tender flower ere its leaves expand. It is the germ on which strong propensities and sentiments are framed. It is in youth that the stronger faculties of the artist, the genius, and the mechanic are pictured. None of these propensities, however, were predominant in my mind while home was my residence. Being the oldest of the boys, my pride was raised to no small degree when I beheld my father preparing a farm for me. This event filled my mind with the grand anticipation of leaving the goats to my brother, who was then beginning to work a little. While my father was making these preparations, I had the constant charge of the goats; and being accompanied by two other boys who resided near my father's house, we wandered many miles from home, by which means we acquired an acquaintance with the different districts of the country. 'Twas while in these rambles with my companions that I became the victim of the slaveholder. While tending our flock between two hills, we spied two men shaping their course towards us. They inquired whether we had any goats for them, a term quite common in that country. Our reply was, of course, in the negative; but they merely used this craft in order to deprive us of suspicion. Myself being nearest to them, I was firmly secured in their hands, and forced away whether I would or not.

On showing symptoms of resistance, one of them procured a green twig, and whipped me till the blood was falling in drops from my legs. After proceeding some miles, we came to a house, where I was tied with ropes hand and foot, and laid down to rest. Next morning, before dawn of day, my cruel master took the ropes off my legs, and, setting me on a certain direction, desired me to walk while he followed with a large whip. Terrified out of my judgment, I saw that there was nothing to be done but either do or suffer. I of course chose the former. This was rather a harsh treatment for a child of eight years of age. Commencing before sunrise, we continued our journey till the middle of the day, when we arrived at a village. This village went under the name of Tegla. At the village of Tegla my inhuman master disposed of me, and returned home. On entering the house of my new master, what was my astonishment on seeing an old acquaintance there, a girl with whom I had an interview a few weeks previous. She, poor creature, had also fallen into the hands of the enemy only a few days before myself. This girl, whose name was Medina, admonished me on this occasion, telling me to do whatever I was desired, assuring me that the white man would not care for taking our lives, that the killing of us would not cost him a thought.

We were well secured with iron chains on our feet, and were never permitted to go far from the house. We could never fall upon plans for effecting our escape, although we often tried different means for that purpose. One night I managed to get the chains off my feet, and would have escaped had not the fear of being recaptured prevented me. Notwithstanding all the plans which Medina resorted to, she could not get the chains off her feet. A short time after this, a caravan (consisting of merchants and travellers) left the village of Tegla. With this caravan our master joined, and, after a day's journey, we arrived at a small village, where he was disappointed in his object, viz., the disposing of us into another's hands, therefore he had no other recourse but to return to his own country. Arriving at the village, we received the heart-rending intelligence that our friends had been in search of us, and were frustrated, having heard that we were taken to a distant land. Another caravan was soon equipped for a farther distance. This was some four days' journey from the village of Tegla, to a large town called Kordofan, under the jurisdiction of the Pacha of Egypt. The first night we pitched our tents at a well of water, not having seen a single house on the whole of our journey. The second day we continued our journey till late at night, when we received the guidance of some light from a distant village, where we arrived and reposed ourselves. This village was called by the natives Albaharr, or, as seen on our maps, Albeit. The inhabitants are a people who might be distinguished among a thousand different nations. Such is their love of jewellery, that they wear rings on their nostrils as well as ears. Instead of horses, or donkeys, or camels, they ride upon bullocks, the noses of which are also adorned with rings, and to these the bridles are tied. We stayed a few days at this place, and shared the unfeigned hospitality of the people, who were uncommonly kind. During our stay here, Medina and I were taken to the camp of the Turks, not far away from the village, where we were put through different exercises. The first thing we were desired to do was to show our tongues, and then our teeth. The rest of our limbs underwent a serious examination also. Having undergone this examination, we were taken back to our lodgings again. The next day our master joined the Turks, who were returning to Kordofan, and by that means ensured our fate of never returning to our native country. In two days we reached the point of our destination, and there our master disposed of us to an Arab, with whom we lived but two or three days. From an Arab we fell into the hands of a Turk. My time while with the first three masters was employed doing nothing. The Turkish gentleman found work for everybody; and all the testimony I can bear to his good character is, that he was one of the cruellest men in existence.

Being an officer of the rank of an aga, his men suffered many harsh cruelties under him. On one occasion, a soldier having been brought to his house for a small offence, he took the office of corporal; and commanding four men to hold him down, beat the poor man, till the blood was running from his cheeks. The keeper of his camels often suffered in a similar way. My office was what might be called a general house-servant. The duties of waiting the table, washing dishes, making coffee, and waiting for orders, were allotted to me as my share of the work. Medina was made assistant cook for a short time, but I had the disagreeable misfortune to see her sold to another Turk; thus I was left to suffer alone.

Some six months, however, relieved me of my hardships. To mention all the cruelties I suffered at that time, would be quite needless. I will only notify a few of them. My master, on whom I had continually to attend, punished every small fault with great severity. If he called, he said I ought to hear him at whatever distance I might be. At one time, being sent from home by my mistress, my master interrogated me on my return with where have you been, and began to thrash me. Self-justification was of no use. No moderate blows did with him, for while he struck one side of my head, he met it at the other side also. I became almost insensible, while the blood was running out of my ears. At another time, having made some coffee by his own orders, I happened to make a few cups more than was required. He said nothing at the time; but after I was in bed, he got hold of a horse whip, and coming upon me unawares, thrashed me till I was quite speechless. I am persuaded he would have killed me had not one of the domestics heard my cries, and come to my rescue. Here I may mention that a very small child can stop a Mahomedan from revenging himself to too great an extent, by taking the whip, or whatever he uses, from him. One of the slaves was the means of preventing my master from whipping me any longer. In Kordofan the houses are all of one storey high. The part in which I lived was chiefly occupied by officers in the Pacha's service. My master was married, had two children, two female slaves, two males, and myself. The other two being grown-up men, were taken out to exercise along with the rest of the soldiers. When coming home from exercise, my master was sure to be heard crying my name a quarter of a mile's distance from the house, at which I had to run out to meet him and carry his sword home. These, and other sufferings of the like nature, prepared me for my subsequent career, and fitted me for the journey on the desert. The circumstances which relieved me of my present master were as singular as the many unlooked-for whippings I received. One evening, when the sun was going down, and everything assuming the quietude of an eastern calm, a certain Arab came to our house, with whom I was desired to go and fetch some soap. I left everything behind me, and went on my supposed errand. Having arrived at the man's house, he asked my name, and told me that I was his property. I merely answered his reply by a look, for ere this time I had become quite regardless of my fate. My new master, whose name was Jubalee, was a native of Dongola, and had come to Kordofan on a trading excursion. He was in company with two others of the names of Auchmet and Mahomet from the same town. Mahomet, the youngest of the two, was a cruel monster, torturing and beating the slaves without any occasion. Auchmet was moderate. My master was of a quiet resigned temper, unless too much interfered with, and very seldom whipped any of his slaves. Having gathered six of us, they now thought of starting for their native country; and to this effect preparations were soon made. They procured four camels, a horse, and other necessaries for travelling, and started, shaping their course to the banks of the Nile. Travelling in these eastern countries is attended with many perilous situations, those engaged in it being exposed to starvation from want of water, liable to be attacked by beasts which have relinquished their first subordination, and entirely under the mercy of the monsoons (a strong wind which raises the sand, by which means many have been buried alive in the eastern deserts).

Our journey (before reaching the banks of the Nile) occupied ten days. Many were the privations we suffered on our way, sometimes from the excessive heat of the sun, and sometimes from want of water. During the middle of the day, we were so much overpowered by the heat, that we often had to delay our journey. At another time we had to exist a whole day without water, under the following circumstances: the water camel, of which I had a particular charge, was going before all the rest, and, unfortunately came upon a dead camel lying on the road. The sight and smell of this animal soon spirit-stirred it, and the result was, that it danced and ran through thick and thin till the water bags, which were hanging on each side of the saddle, were destroyed, having come in contact with some wood on the side of the saddle. Fortune, however, had not altogether turned her face from us, for, in the evening, we came to some wells, where we supplied ourselves and rested for the night. From this place we pursued our journey to the banks of the Nile, and pitched our tents in the valley of Senaar, only a short distance from the town. My master left me here with the old man, two of the slaves, and a camel. Taking with him Mahomet, and the rest of the travelling appendages, he went to the town of Senaar, and there stayed for about a fortnight. During the whole of my time here, I had very little to occupy me, so I ran about through the different places without the least danger of meeting with a second kidnap. The vale at that time was in its prime, the trees having on their coats of variegated green; the grass, the herbs, and flowers, in full bloom; in short, everything was so beautiful, that nature seemed to contradict the wickedness of the world. Happening one day to go to the river side, I observed something uncommon moving on the water, with some white sheets filled with wind, as I thought. I had a dish in which I intended to have carried some water home, but on seeing this curious spectacle approaching me, I took to my heels, and leaving the dish behind, presented myself almost breathless before the old man. On explaining to him the appearance of the sight I had seen, he reprimanded my silliness, and told me that it was a ship, assuring me that it would injure no person, provided the people on board kept quiet, so I went back for my dish. This was the first time I ever saw a ship. My master arriving from Senaar soon after, we started, with an additional number of merchants from the town, and proceeded to Dongola. These merchants were not possessed of slaves, but had a great number of camels, and horses, and donkeys, thus making a formidable caravan. For three or four days we shaped our course along the banks of the Nile, under the direction of one of the native Arabs. At the end of that time, we prepared for a journey on the Libyan desert. Our Arab guide now left us to pilot ourselves, and returned home. I was entirely deprived of a ride on any of the camels, being engaged in leading my old friend, the water camel, which was now turned into an hospital. One of the female slaves having grown ill with a mortal swelling in her thigh, could not walk, and, in consequence, I had to lead the camel on which she rode for nearly a month while crossing the desert. She grew worse and worse every day till she died, and was buried in the sand, without coffin or anything, while her death was not commemorated by the shedding of a single tear. Such are the horrors of the slave trade. Well do I remember the evening of her death. The sun was going down, the azure sky appeared to witness the end with calmness and composure, while the surrounding aspect threw a deep gloom over all our proceedings. I was thrown far behind the rest of the travellers; my fellow companion in slavery began to totter on her saddle, and death was soon announced by her falling from the camel. She was a native of Durfur – a woman in the zenith of her life. The death of this unfortunate female put me in permanent possession of the camel during the remainder of the journey. By this time I became a great favourite with my master; and on one occasion he broke his walking cane over the back of one of the slaves on account of having taken the chief seat on my camel from me. Constrained by sorrow afterwards, my master desired me not to tell how his cane was broken. From the tediousness of our journey, we were glad to see Old Dongola, which predicted our nearness to the point of our destination. This town is situated on the banks of the Nile, and is distinguished for its ruins. We stayed here a short time to recruit our strength, and then proceeded to New Dongola, along the river's banks. A few days saw us home, and on our arrival, the different masters separated, each taking a share of the spoil with him. Auchmet, the eldest, took two of the slaves and a camel; Jubalee took for his share three of the slaves – one having died in the desert; and Mahomet took the rest of the live stock. I was only a few days with my master at his home when I was purchased by Mahomet's father. Mahomet's father and mother were two aged persons, and wished me to be a companion to them while their son followed his occupation. But their next door neighbour having expressed a desire for me to keep his shop, I was accordingly sold to him. I did not like my new master so well as the two former ones – he often behaved cruelly to his slaves. I was generally very fortunate in keeping out of the many whippings which the rest received. On taking me to his house, he gave me some meat, and immediately after took me to his shop, about half a mile from the house. He was a dealer in all sorts of spices and gums – the produce of the country. His shop was in one of the Dongola arcades, and was situated between a doctor's and a jeweller's. Besides myself, another young man, of the name of Salama, graced the shop door. Salama and I became great friends, and often went together to play by the water side. After the shop was shut one evening, we traced our steps, as usual, to the river's side, but what was my singular astonishment on perceiving a female at a distance whom I thought I knew. On going up to her, whom should I see but my old friend, Medina. Salama stood quite astonished when he heard her call me her brother. A small explanation, however, soon settled him. Medina took us to her master's house, and introduced us to her fellows, but our time being limited, we had to leave and get home as quick as possible, promising to return and see them again. This was a thing which we never accomplished while together, for Salama was sold soon after. A few days after this event, Salama and I happened to fall in with a pistol and some powder in the shop. Curiosity induced us to load it. Being the first time I had examined a pistol closely, I desired Salama to fire. He went to the window, and putting the mouth of it out to the open air, fired it off, and loaded it again, asking me to fire it off next. Instead of using the same precautions as he did, I fired it off in the shop, which caused a great smell of powder in the arcade. This induced the neighbours to investigate every place closely, who found that the greatest smell proceeded from our shop. They accordingly took hold of Salama, and would have thrashed him had he not put the blame upon me. I now took to my heels and ran for it, but my limbs were not sufficient to escape so many pursuers in the arcade; in consequence I was captured, and received such a thrashing as I did not forget in a very short time. Luckily our master was away from the shop at the time of this occurrence. Contrary to our expectations, he only gave a laugh when he was informed of our conduct. Soon after our master found out that it was not adequate to keep two of us in the shop, and accordingly sold my friend, Salama. I was now obliged to deal alone among the spices. I made out to pay another visit to Medina, who always gave me a kind reception, and had a little more time to relate our respective histories. I found that I was with my seventh master, whilst she was only with her fifth. Our time being so uncertain, we always bid each other good bye for ever, and it proved so on this occasion. Two or three days after, my master brought a man to the shop, who carefully scrutinized me after the manner of the slave traders, and then I was desired to follow him as my future owner.

Without taking farewell of my fellow slaves who were at the house, I was obliged to abandon everything and follow him. Hemet Hether (for that was the man's name) was a person of a pleasant countenance, a native of Berber, or as it is called by the inhabitants, Barbary. It is a small tract of country lying in the wilds of Upper Egypt, inhabited by a mild race of people, who addict themselves chiefly to agricultural interests. Hemet Hether took me by the hand and led me through the streets of Dongola to the suburbs of the town. We arrived at his brother's house, situated a few miles out of town, where two of his sons were waiting to receive us. I was put into a room where two other slaves were sitting, and with them I soon entered into conversation. The one was a boy the other a girl; the former from Durfur, the latter from Senaar. Our master was merely staying at his brother's for the purpose of gathering slaves, as his home was nearly a month's journey from Dongola, on the way to Cairo, a small village, called by the natives Goortie. Having gathered three of us, he and his sons now thought of going home, and began to prepare accordingly. We started on a morning when the sun was shining on the green fields of corn with bright illumination, and marched along till we found ourselves in a desert country. Before I left Dongola, my old master, Jubalee (having heard that a travelling merchant had bought me), came and gave my character as being an excellent traveller, and mentioned several incidents to ratify that belief on my present master's mind. For this reason I was entrusted with one of the camels. After going through the usual difficulties to be expected in the desert, we arrived at Goortie. The many congratulations which my master received on this occasion were indescribable. His wife kissing him, with tears of joy in her eyes, his daughter clinging to his neck, and the neighbours shaking hands with him, all showed friendship in the superlative degree.

Here I write this small poem:

Tho' Lost to Sight, to Memory Dear

How can the mother's loving eye
Part with the children whom she bore;
Her sons are called, they'll not deny,
To serve on some far distant shore.
Swift time may soar on lofty wing,
With patience yet she'll stand and bear;
She knows they're gone to serve their king,
'Tho' lost to sight, to memory dear.'

How can the loving husband's eye
Look from the wife he holds so dear:
She soon his secrets does descry,
He tells them all without a fear.
But business calls him soon apart,
From her he holds so dear and near;
He ne'er forgets her from his heart,
'Tho' lost to sight, to memory dear.'

But who can mark the sacred glance,
Two lovers bear when doom'd to part;
They part for months, for years, perchance,
Far from those scenes which cheer the heart.
They wait fair fortune's future day,
In hopes to meet some distant year;
Tho' parted far, true love can say,
'Tho' lost to sight, to memory dear.'

Let such as court dear friendship's path,
Pass happy days with friendship here;
Let all forget the way to wrath,
In mutual love let all adhere.
Let those who cherish in their heart
The thoughts – 'Tho' absent, ever dear,'
Remember that although they part,
'Tho' lost to sight, to memory dear.'

The time had not arrived when slave-dealers went to Cairo to dispose of their slaves, in consequence we had to stay at Goortie for three months, during which time I was employed in doing sundry things. First of all, I was sent to live with a friend of my master's, who behaved very kindly to me. Here I had to take care of some cows, while the man's two sons attended to the lands of the farm, which were between three and four miles from the house. About six miles from Goortie, my master married a young woman, with whom I was soon taken to live. In many of the eastern countries, and particularly Egypt, a man is not confined to one wife, but can keep as many as his abilities will allow him. My master's recent marriage was the cause of raising a deal of jealousy on the part of the old one. He chiefly resided at the house he had built for the former, and when the latter met him they were sure to quarrel about something or other. On one occasion, being sent with some corn to the old lady's, on a donkey's back, she would not allow me to empty the sacks, so I had to stand for about half a day to await my master's arrival. On his coming up to me, he asked me why I did not empty the sacks? I told him my reason; after which he went into the house, and a quarrel ensued. The neighbours gathered about the house, and tried to prevent the quarrel; but, my master being in a passion, they found great difficulty in getting him quieted. After he had broken a great number of things, they managed to get him out of the house, and I obtained liberty to empty my sacks and return home. My master also returned to his new wife's, and never went back to Goortie, till within a few days of leaving for Cairo. The slave-ship landed in its season at Goortie, and took us on board. We arrived at the first cataracts of the Nile, and it being impracticable for the ship to proceed farther, we had to change our quarters. The masters busied themselves looking out for another ship to contain their menagerie of human beings. For this purpose we had to travel by land, and finally to sleep on land, before embarking again. Our new ship was a small one, and could not contain all our luggage without a crush; in consequence, some of the slaves sickened, and were paid for their trouble by receiving a good flogging. After a fortnight had elapsed, we landed within a few miles of Cairo, in order to make ourselves look as fresh as daisies before entering the city. From this place we were made to march in military order. The grown up slaves led the van, and I, along with other young ones, marched in the rear, while our masters kept on the flanks. On reaching the entrance to the royal city, we were all counted by a man appointed for that purpose, who found that there were forty of us and ten masters. As soon as the counting was over, each master took his slaves and separated. Our master took us to an acquaintance of his, where he disposed of us, one after the other, but not before two months elapsed. We were regularly taken and exhibited in the slave market, where purchasers came to pick and choose. The grown-up ones soon went off, while the small livestock remained for a long time in the market. A month after, my master shifted to another part of the town, a place near the barracks of Cairo. Here there were several of his countrymen (under the employ of the Pacha) whose duty it was to keep the gate of a manufactory of sundry wares. In this place he left me, and went away, but where I could not tell. A week or ten days after he returned for me, and took me to my old quarter, the slave market, where he soon disposed of me. My ninth master was a European gentleman, of the name of P—. With Mr P— I only lived a fortnight, when I was dispatched (under charge of a Turk) down to Alexandria. The next master into whose hands I fell was R— T—, Esq., British Consul in Egypt. Having fallen into the hands of a British gentleman, I now thought that I was lost, having heard so many Mahommedan prejudices against Christians. Contrary to my expectation, however, I was treated with the greatest clemency, received many indulgences which I never met with before, and what completed my happiness was the pains which Mr L—, my master's son-in-law, took in learning me to read and write. When he found it impossible to teach me himself, the duty devolved upon Mrs S—, the housekeeper. I found much gratification in this novel treatment, and expected to know great things by it. Mrs L, who took great charge of me, never failed in seeing that I was comfortable. While all the African formalities were exchanging for European fashions, four months elapsed, after which the family sailed up the Nile to the first cataracts, taking me, and Mrs S—, and an Italian servant, of the name of Jacquomo. The first cataracts are about 400 miles from Alexandria. A whole month was spent in going and coming back from the cataracts; and the objects which occupied the particular attention of the family were the ancient buildings then standing in ruins. On the left bank of the Nile, and at some distance from Cairo, the Egyptian pyramids present a huge spectacle, having the appearance of small hills. These and many other edifices were built in the distant ages of antiquity, when the Egyptian monarchy flourished under its native dynasty. It is now a country ruled by a despotic viceroy.

The native Egyptians are a quiet, inoffensive people, rather darker than the descendants of Ishmael, and still devote their time to learning, not seeming to have forgot the noble propensities of their ancestors. Architecture had been carried to its highest eminence by the Egyptians three thousand years before the Christian era. The ruins are scattered throughout the whole country. There are several old ruins at the cataracts, and these, along with the waterfalls, form the most romantic scenery imaginable. On our way home, the family visited Thebes and other places of antiquity. Arriving at Alexandria, my master, along with Mr and Mrs L, soon prepared for another journey. Taking Mr and Mrs S— with them, they took the steamer to Malta. This was the first steam-boat I ever had been in, and was curious to know how the vessel went without sails. I asked one of the sailors, who explained the whole mystery by telling me that it went upon wheels. Five days and five nights on the Mediterranean brought us to Malta – a beautiful island, under the British Government. During our quarantine at Lazarett, my master sent Mr and Mrs S—— by a vessel bound for England, while we were confined for three weeks at this place previous to our entering the town. No foreigner is allowed to go to the town of Malta without riding quarantine for a certain length of time. Our time elapsing in this place of confinement, the family went to the town, stayed a short time there, and then set sail for Messina, in Sicily, but the sea grew so boisterous that the vessel (which was but a small one) had to return to Malta again. I had fallen asleep during the night, and was not aware of our return till morning. When I went on deck I learned that the family had gone ashore during the night, while the sailors, who were all Maltese, told me that they were desired to remunerate their toils by appropriating me to themselves. I began to cry, and could not be pacified till they assured me to the contrary. They gave me some breakfast, and two of them (who had received previous instructions) took me to my master.

In a short time after, we again set out to Messina in a larger ship; and, after two days' sail, arrived safe at the long-looked-for place. At Messina my master's nephew (Mr H—— T——) awaited our arrival, and took us to his house. Here we stayed for sometime, and then went to Naples, where my master left Mr and Mrs L——, and proceeded to England. Having left Naples in the evening, the Italian steamer sailed the whole night; and next day, by twelve o'clock, landed us at Leghorn, and there we had to fork for our dinner on shore. Although we were taken on board upon condition of getting everything, they played us the same trick at two other places. When the vessel arrived at Genoa, my master betook himself to inland travelling, wishing to cross the continent, and sail over the channel to England. In pursuance of this scheme, he got a carriage from Genoa to Milan. In the suburbs of Milan my master was met by Mr J—, another son-in-law. After staying a short time here, we left for England. Mr J— also left his family and accompanied my master. We traversed the continent, and permanently crossed the channel from Rotterdam to London.

Having entered Britain, I shall now celebrate the occasion by writing an ode to the country to which many of my countrymen owe their freedom, and liberty of conscience.

Ode to Britain

Surrounded by the foaming surge,
The Queen of land and sea;
For who can boast of Nelson's arms,
Or Wellington's, as thee.

Britain, thou land of peace and joy,
How strong thy bulwarks are;
Thou standest far above the world,
And that without a par.

All nations do thy seamen fear,
Thy ships they see with awe;
Allegiance, too, and homage pay,
As e'er fair Albion saw.

Thy vet'rans prove a fatal scourge,
To those who thee offend;
To those who court thy shelt'ring arms,
Protection dost extend.

Thou wavest high the flag of fame,
Liberty is thy theme,
And while the exile seeks thy shore,
Salvation dost proclaim.

They hail thee as the stranger's home,
The freedom of the slave;
Thy motto is – 'Where'er I go,
The captive I will save.'

The ancient empires, what were they,
When thus compared with thee?
The powers of Media, Greece, and Rome,
Thy fame did never see.

Additional Poems

The Sky

Methinks, when I the world behold,
What things this earth is made to hold,
Creation has not spared her pains,
To show the powers of Him who reigns.

The light blue and transparent sky,
Tells man his mind to lift on high,
And bids him view the ethereal light,
'That beams upon his ravish'd sight.'

The sun, by day, with ardent mirth,
Glows on the cold unfeeling earth:
The moon and stars begin their sway,
And shed their light till morning day.

O look to that palacious view,
Which stands in colours red and blue;
Resign thy fate submissively
To Him who lives above the sky.

No human fiends there can we fear;
No earthly foes above that sphere.
But He who reigns in yonder realm
Wields care's crown with a mercy's helm.

Battle of Gwalior

'Twas when the shades of ev'ning fell
On India's lofty hills of snow:
That eve the minds will ne'er forget
Of those who have escap'd the blow.

'Twas on that eve that Gough did say,
Prepare to fight when e'er you start,

For we will seize Gwalior's fort:
Maharajpoor shall know we're smart.

As soon's the morn began to dawn
Each soldier stood with sword in hand
Resolved to fight with all his might
Or die upon a foreign land.

In columns three they stood array'd
With all their force to face the foe;
From high Gwalior's fort look'd down,
And threw her balls on them below.

Brave Thacwell stood, and at the head
Of the first column did command,
Valiant, with grace, the second took,
While Dennis at the third did stand.

They fought with might and eager true
For Britain's fame and Britain's name,
Till they beheld Maharajpoor
Invested with a fire and flame.

The guns were then to silence called,
Each man to charge with sword in hand
With bay'nets fix'd they did advance,
And shook Gwalior's fort and land.

Gwalior yielded power to them,
Maharajpoor a treaty sign'd,
The British march'd within their bounds,
And left the conquer'd all behind.

Eclipse of the Moon

Led by ambition's mighty force,
A friend and I did take our course
To view the eclipse upon the moon:
We wished to see ere late or soon.

We walked with slow and gentle pace;
Perceived darkness on the moon's trace.
Nought we saw but the cloudy sky;
Nought we heard but the Zephyr's sigh.

All nature lay without alarms,
Wrapt silently in Morpheus' arms.
Nocturnal bliss had lull'd to rest
The chirps of the robin red breast.

While thus our thoughts did wander o'er
Proud nature's wide creative power,
We saw as if reluctantly
The moon peep through the cloudy sky.

Far through the azure of the sky
She stood downcast and ghastly shy.
One minute pass'd and she was gone
Behind her cloudy misty throne.

The Seasons

In winter's freezing frost and wind
How sad the hills and mountains stand,
While ice and snow do fill the plains,
And seal the wide and mighty strand.

The rivers look with mournful gaze;
The hills return their woeful song.
Why does the sun refuse to shine,
And leave us pedling in the throng?

Up starts nature and exclaims,
Why do ye look so sour and sad?
The sun will come and bring again
With him the warm luxuriant plaid.

The voice of spring is heard afar
Proclaim the sun and summer nigh,
While all the birds do sing with joy,
And soar with grace along the sky.

The trees begin to flourish green;
The flowers appear above the ground;
The sun shines with glittering rays,
Diffusing mirth to all around.

Clad with a light translucent robe,
The God of summer glides along.
His 'cheering' breath and 'glad'ning' rays
Give life and health to weak and strong.

See how the stream glides in the vale
To join the sea with rapid pace.
The fruit begins to ripen fast;
The flowers bloom with lovely grace.

But hark! who comes with sheaf of corn
Wrapt round her head with grapes so fine?
Ah! 'tis Pomona in her prime,
Goddess of harvest and the vine.

The winter comes, when she departs;
The spring it bids the birds to sing;
While summer days with mirth return,
Autumnus tries the fruit to bring.

APPENDIX 2

'A Trip up the Congo or Zaire River' by Selim Aga, first published in the *Geographical Magazine*, 1 July 1875

BEFORE STARTING ON an exploratory journey into any part of Africa, it is essential that the traveller should be properly equipped and provided with the necessary kit both for the inward and outward man; clothing, blankets and waterproofs of every description; tea, coffee, and sugar if the latter is desirable; a few bottles of genuine cognac, or some ten-year old Jamaica rum. Well equipped with these necessaries, we started from Fernando Po on the 29th of July for the purpose of ascending the Congo. HMS *Torch* (Captain Smith) took us down to Loango Bay, and there we were transferred to the sloop-of-war *Zebra* (Captain Hoskins), which took us to St Paul's, where we boarded the *Griffon* (Captain Perry). This latter vessel took us to the Congo, and forthwith we commenced a start up the river on the 31st of August. The usual mode of ascending the river as far as Embomma is by means of small fore-and-aft schooners, of about 40 tons burden, which are heavily sparred and well appointed with canvas. Our gear was taken by the *Griffon*'s boats to M Parrat's factory, and there put aboard the French schooner *Esperance*, the native captain of which was a Cabenda man of the name of Frank. We had a fine breeze that afternoon, and the *Esperance* sailed up the river most gallantly. The party on board consisted of Consul Burton, Captain Perry, Mr Bigley, and M Piseaux; a boatswain, four assistant boatswains, captain's servant, the consul's steward Selim, four French native soldiers, and a crew of eight men and boys besides the captain. The following morning we breakfasted at a Portuguese factory, and soon after weighed anchor, and sailed up the river, arriving betimes at Porto da Lenha, and anchored opposite the fine commercial residence of Senhor Monteiro.

On the afternoon of Wednesday (2nd of September) we left Porto da Lenha, and proceeded on our journey, passing several villages. During the night we rounded Point Devil, a most dangerous place for navigation. The following day, about noon, we arrive at Embomma, which contains a French factory and several Portuguese establishments. No white man had been living at the French factory for the last fourteen months, as the emigration system had been abolished. Many of the Portuguese had also deserted their factories, allowing them to decay.

Saturday 5th. The expedition paid a visit to the king of Embomma, and on Sunday we visited Senhor Pereira's gardens, which were very finely laid out, and contained almost every European vegetable. Leaving Senhor Pereira's, at 3.50 p.m., we came to a dangerous bend in the river, where the rocks were visible on the surface of the water, and the current so strong that we had great difficulty in pulling against it. In about two hours we reached the entrance to the creek, which leads to the king of Embomma's village. The reach between this and the Lightning Rock, a little below the European factory, is about 8 miles. At 8.15 we arrived at king Nesalla's village, and having settled an altercation with the canoe-men, who wanted more pay, we made a fresh start.

Early next morning we stopped, and rested till dawn, starting again at 6.30 a.m. The country is hilly, and the river about three-quarters of a mile wide. After journeying for two hours we halted and breakfasted near the Alecto Rock, so-called from some of the 'Alecto's' men having painted a white trident on it. At 9.30 we again got under weigh, and soon entered a part of the river where it assumes the appearance of an inland lake, some parts being nearly two miles wide. Near the upper end are two islands, the lower of which is very small, and has a single large tree growing upon it, which makes it very picturesque. The scenery here is varied, but principally hilly, the highest of the hills being about 1,500 feet above the level of the river. Opposite the tree island we met a native chief in his canoe. He came to levy contributions from us. His people, who were armed with guns and matchlocks, made various warlike gestures, and ordered us to stop. M Piseaux, being our guide and adviser, we were compelled to pay one bottle of rum, and a piece of cloth 12 fathoms in length. The grass was dry all over the hills, that close to the water's edge being an exception; and very little animal life was perceptible, consequently the country presented a very barren and desolate appearance. Most of the trees were stunted and leafless, the chief of them being the baobob or monkey-bread tree, the fan-palm or Palmyra, a few palm-nut trees, and a species of large spreading tree well scattered over the shores, the leaves of which are of a dark green colour, about the size of the lime leaf, and its fruit a long reddish plum, said to be eaten by monkeys. In the afternoon we arrived at another opening in the river, which extended and widened some 3 or 4 miles to the left, and was apparently hemmed in by a very high range of hills. This was the limit of M Piseaux's knowledge of the river, and, to our future sorrow and vexation, we landed in the banza or district of Nokki.

Next day (Tuesday, September 8th) we journeyed into the interior, and found the road excessively irksome and trying; nothing but hills and dales. Passing one or two fields of native beans, we arrived at the village of Kindemba, have crossed two places where water was procurable, the one a running stream, and the other a spring oozing out of the ground close to some rocks. After resting here for a short time we ascended a hill some 600 or 700 feet in height, and came to another village, where we saw something like a large baracoon for slaves, but which turned out to be a fetish house for circumcised boys. Not many minutes walk from this is the village of Kayé, on entering which all our things were put down, and we were marched off to see his majesty the king of this part of the country. We found him seated in state, dressed up in motley garb of European manufacture, a white shirt with collar turned down, a crimson velvet loin cloth fringed with gold, tied round the waist by means of a belt; a beautifully mounted sheath knife was stuck in his belt, the handle of which was made of nickel silver, being very showily ornamented with imitation emeralds and ruby garnets. Over all his dress was a beadle's red cloak, and on his head a helmet something resembling those worn by English

Life Guardsmen; but it was evidently of French manufacture. The king was very young, apparently not more than twenty years of age, and very shy. When the strangers were seated, one on a chair, and the other two on a covered table, the rest of the courtiers sat down on the ground at a respectful distance both from the strangers and the throne. The king's old father was also there, on the ground before his son. The king's name was Sudikil, and that of his father, Mavonga. After the interview, Sudikil received his presents, with which he expressed dissatisfaction, and would give us nothing to eat, consequently Captain Perry, with Dean and M Piseaux, at once started for the river to return to Embomma. The consul engaged Nchama, a native who spoke African idiomatic Portuguese, to act as interpreter and go-between. Our party when it first started from the river, consisted of fifty-six persons, but as soon as we arrived at Kindemba it began to augment, and on our arrival at Kayé it had reached to 150. We were domiciled in the house of Chico Mpambo, a man who put himself up as a French interpreter, but who really knew nothing whatever of that language.

Early next morning we received a visit from Gidi Mavonga and his son Sudikil, who examined all our travelling gear. After half an hour's palaver everything was handed over to Gidi, who promised to start for the Congo in three days, and in consideration of receiving the said goods, bound himself to take us there, bring us back, and feed us by the way. This arrangement was very good, as it secured the friendship of the old chief, besides preventing him or his people from robbing or poisoning us. This day we received a visit from Tetu Mayella, king of an adjacent village, called Neprat. He was accompanied by about twenty followers, all of whom came to us for the express purpose of getting some rum. After a deal of wrangling, Tetu and party received a bottle of gin, for which he presented us with two fowls. This was a godsend, as the day before we had nothing to eat but a few pieces of dry bread. About the same time a pig was brought and slaughtered with great ceremony. Final arrangements were made at last with Gidi to proceed at first to Yellala, or the Congo cataracts, and afterwards to St Salvador, or Great Congo City. The direction of the Yellala cataracts from the village of Kayé is ENE and that of St Salvador or Congo, ESE.

About noon next day (Thursday, September 10th) we commenced packing in order to start for Gidi Mavonga's village. The natives of Congo are divided into two classes only, the Mfumo, or freeman, and the Muleque, or slave. The Mfumo marries among his own slaves, or, properly speaking retainers, and the children born to him are in their turn Mfumos, or free men. The word slave here is quite improperly used, for the slave is, in reality, a freer man than the prince himself. Everything the prince possesses, except his wives, is literally at the disposal of the slave. Unquestionably, the slave is the body-guard of the Mfumo, but as regards work he does what he likes, sleeps when he chooses, attends to his own private affairs whenever he pleases, and if his master finds fault with his conduct, the chances are, if his own country is not too far away from the place of his thraldom, he will leave him and make an effort to reach the place that gave him his birth.

Gidi Mavonga came next morning to take us to his village, which we reached in half an hour. The only object of interest passed on he way was a palm-tree which the lightning had struck, killing it and tearing up several feet of ground. This was the first time we had seen any mischief done by lightning in West Africa. Gidi appeared to be a great worshipper of the native fetish. Mavunga is a consecrated country pot, and is placed in a small hut at the entrance to the town, and is supposed to be the presiding genius or patron saint of the place in which it is worshipped. Ibamba or Mzamba is a representation of Diabulus. The natives call him Masjinga, and is a house god, usually keeping guard at the bedside. The one at Gidi's house was a peculiarly droll looking object, about 3 feet in height, with mouth wide open, his under lip hanging down, the upper lip drawn up, as if by some strong convulsion, nose flat, and the nostrils very much inflated. His eyes were composed of pieces of looking glass, and a piece was also inserted in his belly, but for what purpose we could not find out. On his head was an English billy-cock hat, and round about his shoulders hung different kinds of medicines, a calabash and kind of knife. The face of this wonderful figure was black, red, and white.

About mid-day we were visited by some neighbouring chiefs, all gaily attired as usual. They wore common red night caps on their heads, and this was the only head-dress we ever saw adopted by the men on great occasions, Sudikil's military helmet excepted. The women always go bareheaded. We have often wondered where in all the wide universe the whole of our old clothes go after they are purchased by the Jews in the streets of London. The mystery is solved without much difficulty, for we found kings wearing old second-hand livery vests, with the coronet of a marquis on the button; and princes sporting their figures dressed in old livery coats and marines' jackets of the last century; besides a variety of heterogenous habiliments, such as old superfine black coats which had been worn threadbare, and pantaloons the seats of which had become quite glazed from long service. All these had been cleaned and turned inside out by the Jews; and although some of the textures would scarcely bear the tug of a common needle and thread, they are all sent out to the West Coast of Africa as brand new garments, love of dress entirely blinding the natives from observing the various defects. After regaling our visitors with palm-wine and a bottle of gin, they went away.

The chief Furano, who was expected from Embomma, arrived next morning (Saturday, September 12th), and we at once started for the cataracts. After marching for a short time, and passing two or three small villages, we commenced a rapid descent in a NNE direction, and journeying at a rapid place for about 3 miles we entered the village of Chinsawu, the residence of Prince Nelongo. On arriving at Nelongo's we had to wait half an hour on the verandah of an empty house before we were honoured by the presence of his highness, who intimated his pleasure of seeing us by asserting that unless the same presents were given to him as were given to Sudikil, it would be impossible for us to pass his place. This was too preposterous, for we only stopped here to breakfast, whereas we were four or five days in the territory of Sudikil. At 11:15 my master arranged some botanical specimens which he had collected on the road and I cut the letter B and 1863 on the trunk of a large *Adansonia* or baobab-tree in this village.

We got comfortably house in Nelongo's village, where we noticed as we did in other places on the banks and neighbourhood of the Congo, that the children were all afraid of the white man; for when any one attempted to bring them close to the consul, the little brats howled as if Ajax from the infernal regions had got hold of them.

The whole of the next morning (Sunday) was taken up satisfying Nelongo, the native idea of the quantity of goods the white man possessed being quite fabulous. At noon we again made a start, the sun being very hot, the thermometer standing at 90 degrees in the shade. We made a slight descent into a valley, and then ascended a peculiarly formed hill, from the summit of which we obtained a glorious view of the river, which was seen some 800 feet below us, flowing down rapidly and majestically to the sea; but the utter barrenness of the country in the vicinity of its banks carried away every association of fertility from the mind of the lover of the commixture of all the elements which constitute the four seasons. This view of the country, however, is given at the end of the dry season, when almost every tree is leafless, and the grass is withered.

From this point commenced a decline downhill which baffles description. We had walked on and lost sight of the river, and the second time we sighted it we had not journeyed quarter of a mile before we arrived at a part of our road where, without exaggeration, the path, if such it could be called, was only two degrees from the perpendicular, and as slippery as ice, owing to the quantity of loose stones and dry grass that lay everywhere.

The distance from Nelongo to the banks of the river is about 5 miles, and on reaching the waterside we found ourselves at exactly at the junction of the Nomposo with the Congo River. The Nomposo, we were informed, extends all the way to St Salvador, but is not navigable even for canoes. There were some fishermen following their vocation at the mouth of this small river, whose services we brought into requisition to take us across and land us a little above its mouth, but on the banks of the great river. There are two rock islands in the river, on both of which there are some tall green shrubs. On the opposite bank is the Banza Vivi, the best place on the river for anyone to land wishing to see the cataracts of the Banza Nculu. This is generally about the season when the light or dry season rains commence, and which usually last about six weeks or two months, and are a great boon to the natives, who depend on corn for subsistence. Maize or Indian corn can be grown in about forty days. An intelligent farmer, who can command water, will easily grow three crops a year. Cotton comes to perfection in four months, rice ditto and cabbages between three and four months; casada – good for starch or arrowroot – from six to nine months; plantains and bananas, once a year; radishes, three weeks to a month; turnips in two months, and lettuces, endive, and carrots, from three to four months. The cultivation of peas is not only a loss of time, but a waste of ground, for they never bear enough in two rows, 12 feet by 4, to make a good plateful.

It is always advisable, in travelling through Africa, to keep guides and interpreters from knowing what you are really possessed of, for they are sure to make some excuse to fleece you. This morning (Monday, September 14th) we had evidence of the foregoing. We had paid our guide everything that was requisite for the road, yet, notwithstanding this, he sent the interpreter to ask us for a piece of fancy cloth, which they knew we had in our possession. You must grant their request, otherwise you may have to give up your journey, for, ten chances to one, they will leave you. Having crossed the river we waited for Gidi and a few hands that had been left behind. On their arrival we started for Vivi, and reached the village after half-an-hour's march.

The king of Vivi, Nesalla by name, spoke Portuguese, and sent us three bunches of plantains and seven fowls for the expedition. In the afternoon, Nesalla came with upwards of one hundred armed men, and commenced a long palaver about our going on to the Yellalla. Five or six persons spoke, and the conference lasted an hour. The result was that the cloth we had with us was not enough, and that the princes at Yellalla must get a different piece from that which was before the conference, and no division into two pieces was to be made of it under any consideration whatsoever. As the whole affair was conducted in a good-humoured manner my master agreed to the terms. In the evening the inhabitants of the village had a dance, which ended in drunkedness and uproar.

Banza Vivi, like all other parts of the country, is entirely free from bush. The inference to be drawn from this fact is that the whole country, at no very remote period, must have been under cultivation. In trade the natives always give full measure; and in filling a jug with palm-wine it is always done to overflowing. A circumstance illustrative of this took place whilst we were staying at Senhor Peireira's at Embomma. A bag of ground-nuts was being measured, and the vendor finding that the measure did not overflow, at once ran to the market, and returned with the requisite quantity to make up the quantum.

Early next morning (Tuesday, September 15th) we started for the Banza Nculu. The scenery along the road was varied and picturesque. The first view we had of the river was from an eminence about a mile from Vivi. Here we had a view of the Congo as it was flowing onwards, and round about in all directions were hills and dales of various sizes, adding a panoramic beauty to the scene, far beyond the conception of an artist's pencil. We had to descend from the summit of this hill, and ascend a second one much higher, from which we again obtained views of the Congo. One, the lower view, appeared like a lake apparently shut in on all sides by hills, the lofty summits of which, stretching far and wide on every side, and some of them peering to the height of above 10,000 feet into the heavens, gave the appearance of Dr Johnson's ideal Happy Valley of *Rasselas*. Proceeding onwards, we ascended a third eminence, but by this time we had entirely lost sight of the river, and our path became more level for a short distance. Stopping to gather some flowers, I lost sight of the last of the carriers, and it was some time before I found them. On entering a small village, I espied them surrounded by natives – men, women and children, all of whom appeared to be highly delighted at the sight of the white men.

We now commenced a gradual descent, but before doing so we obtained an open and extensive view of the valley that lay between us and Banza Nculu.

On descending into the valley, we found the soil a dark clay mould, with fewer stones than that of the country through which we had hitherto passed. It was certainly a fine sight to behold, and the best addition to the scene was the caravan forming the expedition, now disappearing down a valley, now rising to the top of one of the many hillocks with which the valley abounds. The fertility of the soil may be observed here from the fact of the grass growing to the height of 10 to 12 feet. And here, also, the native beans grow to a greater height than those met with in other parts of the country. In the valley we crossed three streams – all feeders of the big river – and, considering it was the close of the dry season, these streams had a fair supply of water.

We now arrived at the summit of Banza Nculu Hill, where we had to wait the pleasure of the three kings, who with their interpreters were settling some business. So we had to bivouac under a large tree until their highnesses condescended to grant us an audience. Bearing due south from this tree, and on the left bank of the river, is Palabala, one of the many ways by which a traveller may reach Sundi, above the Congo Rapids, where the rivers is said to become deep, broad and navigable.

About two o'clock one of the interpreters was sent to put us into a house. In an hour and a half's time we heard the beating of drum and cone (an instrument similar to the triangle), and on looking out a procession was seen wending its way to our new lodgings. The three ministers of the kings were the principal personages, and had come as ambassadors from their master. After three conferences the moderate sum of £300, in cloth beads and liquor, was demanded, in order to continue our journey to Sundi, a distance of only three days' march.

Our object was to reach Sundi, and from thence try to ascertain the course of the river, and to find out whether its source could be reached by canoes or carriers, but finding the demands of the chiefs beyond our power of compliance, we at once resolved to return. Before doing so, however, we proceeded next day to view the Yellalla Rapids, which run ENE and WSW and may be said to be about a mile in length. They are assuredly very grand, although the natives led us to expect something even grander. Some fishermen were busy catching fish up and down the quieter parts of the rapids, while the eagles and cranes were satisfying their hunger in the vicinity of the island of Sanga-Cha-Malemba in the middle of the stream.

All day Gidi Mavonga was very stubborn and irritable, wishing to start at once for Vivi, and return home; but my master having to arrange some botanical specimens, to finish two sketches of this part of the country, and being foot-sore, would not hear of starting.

September the 19th found us again at Gidi's village, paying off all the extra hands who had accompanied us to the rapids; and on the 24th we were once more at Embomma, arriving at Porta da Lenhaon the 26th. Next day at 4.15 a.m. we arrived at Point Banana, and at 6 o'clock all our things were landed and comfortably housed in M Parrat's factory.

Selim Aga

APPENDIX 3
Timeline of Events Associated with the Lives of Selim Aga and Richard Burton

1807	Abolition of the Slave Trade Act passed by the British Parliament
1820	Egyptian Pasha Muhammed Ali conquers Sudan
1821	Birth of Richard Francis Burton
*c.*1827	*Birth of Selim Aga*
1822	Slaves freed in Liberia
1830–32	Lander brothers travel down the Niger from Bussa to its mouth
1833	Slavery abolished in British Colonies
*c.*1835	*Selim captured as slave*
*c.*1836	*Selim released from slavery and travels to Scotland*
1842	Burton arrives in India as army officer
1846	Incidents in the Life of Selim Aga *published in Aberdeen*
1849	*Selim takes up residence in London*
1849	Burton returns to England on sick leave
1849–55	Heinrich Barth travels from Tripoli to Chad and Timbuctoo and back
1851	Great Exhibition in London
*c.*1853	*Selim presents his* Africa Considered in its Social and Political Condition, with a Plan for the Amelioration of its Inhabitants *to the Foreign Office*
1853	Burton, in disguise, travels to the holy city of Mecca
1854	William Baikie's first journey up the Niger River
1855	Burton travels to the forbidden city of Harar in Somalia
1857	*Selim travels on Dr William Baikie's second expedition up the Niger*
1858	Burton accompanied by William Hanning Speke are

	first Europeans to discover Lake Tanganyika
1859	Burton arrives in London to find that Speke has claimed discovery of source of Nile
1860	Burton travels in Canada and USA and describes Mormon society
1861	Britain annexes Lagos
1861	Burton marries Isabel Arundell and takes up consular duties at Fernando Po
1861	*Selim taken on as manservant to Richard Burton and accompanies him to Cameroon Mountains*
1862	*Selim accompanies Burton on gorilla hunt in the Gabon*
1862	*Selim accompanies Burton to Wari and Benin*
1863	*Selim accompanies Burton up the Congo*
1863	*Selim accompanies Burton to Dahomey*
1864	Burton leaves Fernando Po for England and becomes Consul in Santos, Brazil
1869	Suez Canal opened
1869	Burton appointed to consulship at Damascus, which he held until 1871
1872	Burton appointed consul at Trieste
1875	*Death of Selim*
1882	British occupy Egypt
1885–88	Burton publishes *The Book of the Thousand Nights and a Night,* regarded as his finest literary work
1890	Death of Sir Richard Burton

APPENDIX 4
The Thurburn Family

ON JOHN THURBURN'S death, his estate passed to his wife, Elizabeth, with provisions for their daughter Anna to receive the income from the estate. Anna married William Osborne MacLaine in 1849 with provision for a marriage settlement of £20,000. Thurburn's grandson, John Thurburn Maclaine, the second of Anna's sons – the first, Hector Maclaine (b.1857) was killed in 1880 in the Afghan Wars – was designated heir on Anna's death in 1882, aged fifty-eight. After her husband's death, Anna remarried to a Mr Richardson Cox. At the time of Thurburn Maclaine's marriage in 1881 (to RH Miller), he is described as the 'younger of Kyneton' being in the district of Thornbury, Gloucestershire, where the Maclaine family had their estate.

The graves of John Thurburn, his wife, and daughter Barbara, are in Peterculter Parish Churchyard, a few miles west of Aberdeen. The youngest of Robert Thurburn's sons, Captain Henry Thurburn, lived in Muchalls in Aberdeenshire, following his service in India, and died in 1897.

There are a substantial number of estate papers lodged in Aberdeen University library, but these are mainly post-1850 and make no reference to Selim. Robert died in 1860 and was buried at Lyons in France. John Thurburn Maclaine died in 1892.

After the death of Elizabeth Thurburn in 1872, the Murtle estate was sold and passed though a number of hands, until it was purchased by the Camphill Rudolf Steiner Schools in 1942. Although the original house, now a Listed Building, still stands, it has been considerably altered internally, while the extensive grounds have been developed for accommodation for the pupils of the school.

Bibliography

Unpublished Sources

Aberdeen University Special Collections: Thurburn Family Papers.
Scottish Wills
Bock, F: *History of Murtle* (unpublished, 1998)
Fraser, GM: *Notes and Jottings* nd vol 43, P25, Aberdeen Central Library
Historic Scotland Register of Listed Buildings, Aberdeenshire Area, nd
Kew Gardens Archives: Director's Correspondence related to Gustav Mann, folios 291, 387–90
Murtle Estate Papers, 1861–91, Aberdeen University, AU MS 2769
National Archives: Foreign Office Correspondence with British Consuls in West Africa 1861–64 (FO 2/40; 2/42; 2/45; 8/117; 8/1147; 84/1176; 84/1203; 84/1221)
Reid, T: Information on British Censuses of 1841, 1851,1861, & 1871 (*personal communication*)
Thurburn Family Notes per Andrew Thurburn (*personal communication*)
Walls, Marion: Information on descendants of Selim Aga (*personal communication*)

Published Sources

Except where otherwise stated, publication is in London and where original and later editions are both given, the latter has been used for references to page numbers in end notes.

Aberdeen Journal, 6 February 1861: John Thurburn (obituary)
Adams, DG: *Bothy Nichts and Days: Farm Bothy Life in Angus and the Mearns*, Edinburgh, 1992
Aga, S: *Incidents Connected with the Life of Selim Aga, A Native of Central Africa*, Aberdeen, 1846; London, 1850
–*Africa Considered in its Social and Political Condition with a Plan for the Amelioration of its Inhabitants*, 1853
–'My Parentage and Early Career as a Slave' *Geographical Magazine,* May, 1874, 63–9
–'A Trip up the Congo or Zaire River' *Geographical Magazine,* 1 July 1875, 203–07

Altick, RD: *The Shows of London,* 1978
Asher, M: *In Search of the Forty Days Road*, 1984
–*A Desert Dies*, New York, 1986
Barbour, KM: *The Republic of the Sudan*, 1961
Bowring, J: *Report on Egypt 1823–1838 Under the Reign of Mohammed Ali*, 1998 (originally published as *Report on Egypt and Candia*, 1840)
Brodie, FM: *The Devil Drives,* 1967
Burckhardt, JL: *Travels in Nubia*, 1819
Burne, GS: *Richard Burton*, Boston, 1985
Burton, RF: *Personal Narrative of a Pilgrimage to El-Medina and Meccah*, 1855
–*Proceedings of the Royal Geographic Society*, 1862, 239
–*Abeokuta and the Cameroons Mountains*, 2 vols, 1863(a)
–'My Wanderings in West Africa: A Visit to the Renowned Cities of Weri and Benin', *Fraser's Magazine*, February 1863 (b)
–*Mission to Gelele, King of Dahome*, 1866
–*Two Trips to Gorilla Land and the Cataracts of the Congo*, 1876
Cameron, DA: *Egypt in the Nineteenth Century*, 1898
Casada, A J: *Sir Richard F. Burton: A Biobibliographical Study*, 1990
Cay, W & Sons: *In Memoriam: An Obituary for Aberdeen and Vicinity*, 1997
Cooke, N: 'James Burton and Slave Girls', *Unfolding the Orient: Travellers in the Near East* (eds) Starkey, P & J, 2001
Cooper, Merian, C: 'Two Fighting Tribes of the Sudan', *National Geographic*, October 1929, 464–86
Cormack, AA: *Education in the Eighteenth Century: Parish of Peterculter, Aberdeen*, Banff, 1965
Crowther, S & Taylor, JC: *The Gospel on the Banks of the Niger*, 1859, 1968
Crowther, S: *Journal of an Expedition up the Niger and Tshadda Rivers*, 1855, 1970
Denham, Clapperton and Oudney:*Travels and Discoveries in North and Central Africa*, 1826
Elles, RJ: 'The Kingdom of Tegali', *Sudan Notes & Records*, XVIII, 1935, 1–35
Ereira, A: *The People's England*, 1981
Ewald, Janet J: *Soldiers, Traders and Slaves: State Formation and Economic Transformation in the Greater Nile Valley, 1700–1885*, Wisconsin, 1990
Faris, JC: 'Nuba' in Weekes, RV (ed) *Muslim Peoples: A World*

Ethnographic Survey, 1984
Farwell, B: *Burton*, 1963
Fleming, F: *The Sword and the Cross*, 2003
Forbes, FE: *Dahomey and the Dahomans: Being the journals of two missions to the King of Dahomey, and residence at his capital in the years 1849 and 1850*, 1851
Forster, EM: *Alexandria: A History and Guide*, 1982
Fraser, WH & Morris, RJ: *People and Society in Scotland, 1830–1914*, Edinburgh, 1990
Gershoni, Y: *The Americo-Liberian Scramble for the Hinterland*, 1985
Gliddon, GM: *Handbook to the American Panorama of the Nile*, 1849
Glover, ER: *Life of Sir John Hawley Glover*, 1879
De Gramont, S: *The Strong Brown God: The Story of the Niger River*, 1975
Grant, E: *Memoirs of a Highland Lady*, Edinburgh 1898
Grant, J: *History of the Burgh and Parish Schools of Scotland*, Glasgow, 1876
Grant, JA: 'Route March, with Camels, from Berber to Korosco in 1863', *Proceedings of the Royal Geographic Society* vi, 326–25, 1884
Glover, Lady: *Life of Sir John Hawley Glover*, 1897
Gray, R: *A History of the Southern Sudan 1839–1889*, 1961
Gregor, Rev W: *An Echo of the Olden Time*, 1874
Grindlay, RM: *Hints for Travellers to India*, 1847
Guannu, JS (ed): *A Short History of the First Liberian Republic*, 1885
Haldane, E: *The Scotland of our Fathers: A Study of Scottish Life in the Nineteenth Century*, Glasgow, 1933
Halls, JJ: *Life and Correspondence of Henry Salt*, 1834
Hamilton, E: *Life on a Country Estate in the Mid Nineteenth Century*, Dugdale Society Occasional Papers, 1991
Hare, J: *Shadows Across the Sahara*, 2001
Hastings, ACG: *The Voyage of the Dayspring*, 1926
Hastings, M. *Sir Richard Burton*, 1987
Hawkesworth 'The Nuba Proper of Southern Kordofan', *Sudan Notes and Records*, vol xv (2), 1932
Henderson, JA: *History of the Parish of Banchory-Devenick*, Aberdeen, 1890
–*Annals of Lower Deeside*, Aberdeen, 1892
Hendrie, WF: *The Dominie: A Profile of the Scottish Headmaster*, Edinburgh, 1997

Hill, R: *On the Frontiers of Islam: Two Manuscripts Concerning the Sudan under Turco-Egyptian Rule 1822–1845*, Oxford, 1970
Hillelson, S: 'Nubian Origin' *Sudan Notes and Records*, vol XIII (1), 1930
Hogg, E: *Visit to Alexandria*, 2 vols, 1835
Holroyd, AT: *In Bowring*, 1840
Holt, PM & Daly: *A History of the Sudan*, 1979
Holt, PM: *History of the Sudan*, 2000
Hoskins, HL: *British Routes to India*, 1928
Howard, C: *West African Explorers*, 1951
Jeal, T: *Livingstone*, 1973
Jutzi, AH: *In Search of Sir Richard Burton*, San Marino, 1993
Kenrick, JW: 'The Kingdom of Tegali 1921–1946', *Sudan Notes & Records*, vol XXIX (2), 1948, 143–50
Lach-Szyrma, Krystyn: *From Charlotte Square to Fingal's Cave: Reminiscences of a Journey through Scotland 1820–1824*, East Linton, 2004
Lowell, MS: *A Rage to Live: A Biography of Richard and Isabel Burton*, 1998
Luz, Oskar: 'Proud Primitives: The Nuba People', *National Geographic*, November 1966, 672–99
McCarthy, J: *Journey into Africa: The Life and Death of Keith Johnston*, Latheronwheel, 2004
–'Connecting the Lakes: Two Scottish Pioneers', *The Society of Malawi Journal* vol 57 (2) 2004
MacMichael, HA: *A History of the Arabs in the Sudan*, vol 1, Cambridge, 1922
Madden, RR: *Travels in Turkey, Egypt, Nubia and Palestine*, 1829
–*Egypt and Mohammed Ali*, 1841
Madox, J: *Excursions in the Holy Land, Egypt, and Syria*, 1834
Mathew, HCG: & Harrison, B (eds): *Oxford Dictionary of National Biography*, Oxford, 2004
Mountfield, D: *A History of African Exploration*, 1976
Nachtigall, G: *Sahara and Sudan II*, 1885, Berlin, 1971
Nadel, SF: *The Nuba: An Anthropological Study of the Hill Tribes of Kordofan*, Oxford, 1947
Nazer, Mende: *Slave: The True Story of a Girl's Lost Childhood and her Fight for Survival*
Naulty, DN: *Dundee Cinemas*, Dundee, 2004

New Statistical Account of Scotland, 1845
Northcroft, D: *Scots at School: An Anthology*, Edinburgh, 2003
Pallme, I: *Travels in Kordofan*, 1844
Petherick, J: *Egypt, the Soudan, and Central Africa*, 1861
Saeed, AAR: in Rahhal, Suleiman Musa (ed): *The Right to be Nuba: The Story of a Sudanese People's Struggle for Survival*, 2000
Udal, JO: *The Nile in Darkness: Conquest and Exploration 1504–1862*, 1998
Underhill, EB: *Alfred Saker: A Biography*, 1884
Rocco, F: *The Miraculous Fever Tree*, 2003
Sagar, JW: 'Notes on the History, Religion, and Customs of the Nuba', *Sudan Notes and Records*, vol v, December 1922
Schonfield, HJ: *Richard Burton: Explorer*, 1936
Scott, CR: *Rambles in Egypt and Candia*, 1837
Seaman, LCB: *Life in Victorian London*, 1973
Segal, R: *Islam's Black Slaves*, 2001
Stevenson, RC: *The Nuba People of Kordofan Province: An Ethnographic Survey*, Khartoum, 1984
Strachan, Robin: 'With the Nuba Hillmen of Kordofan', *National Geographic*, February 1951, 249–78
Thurburn, FAV: *The Thurburns*, 1864
Toniolo, E & Hill, R: *The Opening of the Nile Basin*, 1974
de Vries, L (ed): *The World of the Early Victorians as Seen through the Eyes of the Illustrated London News*, 1967
Wilkins, WH (ed): *Wanderings in Three Continents*, 1901
Wright, T: *Life of Sir Richard Burton*, 1906

References

INTRODUCTION
Searching for Selim

1. The original reference in *Queen* magazine has not been found
2. Aga, (1874) *passim*
3. Burton, (1875) 203–04
4. Burton, (1862) 239
5. Burton, (1875) 204
6. Bock, 3

CHAPTER ONE
The Kingdom of Taqali

1. Aga, (1874) 67–68
2. Aga, (1846) 12–13
3. Holt, 5
4. Saheed, 18
5. Aga, (1846) 6–7
6. Aga, (1846) 14
7. Barbour, 174
8. Ewald, 18
9. Pallme, 171–75
10. Toniolo & Hill, 29
11. Saeed, 11
12. Ewald, 30–31
13. Pallme, 170
14. Elles, 12
15. Ewald, 85–86
16. Pallme, 175
17. Elles, 1–2
18. Toniolo & Hill, 285
19. Pallme, 172
20. Elles, 3
21. Aga, (1874) 66
22. Aga, (1874) 63
23. Toniolo & Hill, 293
24. Pallme, 172
25. Elles, 21
26. Aga, (1874) 67–68
27. Aga, (1874) 68
28. Pallme, 173–75
29. Aga (1846) viii

CHAPTER TWO
'A thing to be bartered for'

1. Aga (1874) 64
2. Asher, 39
3. Ewald, 34
4. Pallme, 258–73
5. *Ibid*, 202
6. Aga, (1874) 5
7. Pallme, 270–72
8. Holroyd, 86–87
9. Aga (1874) 64
10. *Ibid*, (1846) 22–23

CHAPTER THREE
The Nile Journey

1. Grant, J, 326
2. Toniolo & Hill, 305
3. Aga, (1874) 68
4. *Ibid*, (1874) 68
5. Holt & Daly, 9–10
6. Denham, 145
7. Aga, (1846) 26
8. Toniolo & Hill, 306–37
9. Fleming, 120–21
10. Toniolo & Hill, 278–79
11. Aga, (1846) 28
12. Hare, 76
13. Aga, (1874) 68
14. *Ibid*, 69

15. *Ibid*, (1846) 22
16. *Ibid*, 69
17. *Ibid*, (1874) 69

CHAPTER FOUR

'The fate of the author was sealed'

1. Segal, 1–36
2. *Ibid* 40–41
3. Nachtigall, 103
4. Holroyd, 486–87
5. Segal, 56
6. Holroyd, 239
7. Segal, 150
8. Nachtigall, 653
9. Holroyd, 480
10. Cooke, 1–3
11. Holroyd, 480 *et seq*
12. Segal, 62
13. Bowring, 233
14. Pallme, 326 *et seq*
15. Elles, 17
16. Aga, (1846) x

CHAPTER FIVE

Robert Thurburn of Alexandria

1. Bowring, 17–18, 296–299
2. Thurburn, *mss* 52 *et seq*
3. Halls, 276–80
4. Thurburn, *mss* 58
5. Thurburn *mss*, 63
6. Bowring, 296
7. Thurburn, *mss* 67
8. Madden, 56 *et seq*
9. Thurburn, *mss* 68
10. Hogg, 123, 127
11. Udal, 358
12. Burckhardt, lxxv
13. Petherick, 3–4
14. Udal, 383–410
15. Grindlay, 74
16. Hoskins, 221–37
17. Thurburn, *mss* 69
18. Aga, (1846) iii
19. Lowell, 121–22
20. Wright, 235
21. Thurburn, *mss* 74

CHAPTER SIX

'The comforts of a civilised and social life'

1. Historic Scotland Register of Listed Buildings, Aberdeenshire
2. Murtle Estate Papers
3. Thurburn, FAV, 16
4. Henderson, 204–11
5. Murtle Estate Papers
6. Aga, (1846) end paper
7. *Aberdeen Journal*, 5 Feb 1861
8. Aga, (1876) iii
9. Haldane, 110–18
10. Haldane, 295
11. Smout, (1990) 16
12. Haldane, 119–20
13. Smout, (1990) 90 *et seq*
14. Adams, *passim*
15. Fraser, 52
16. Aberdeenshire Census, 1841
17. Smout, (1990) 95
18. Lach-Szyrma, 101
19. Smout, (1990) 95
20. Aberdeen Census, 1851
21. Smout, (1990) 13

CHAPTER SEVEN

'They hail thee as the stranger's home'

1. Aberdeenshire Census, 1851
2. Haldane, 38–40
3. *Aberdeen Journal*, 5 Feb 1861
4. Bock, 3
5. Cay, 234–35
6. Bock, 3
7. Gregor, 1
8. Aberdeenshire Census, 1851
9. Burton, (1875) 204
10. Anderson, R, in Northcroft, 18
11. Smout, (1999) 57
12. Grant, J, *passim.*
13. Hendrie, 34
14. Northcroft, 31
15. Burton, (1875) 204
16. Lach-Szyrma, 137
17. Aga, (1846) 39
18. Aga, (1853) 8
19. Burton, (1875) 204

CHAPTER EIGHT

'A key to the civilisation of the whole world'

1. Seaman, 9
2. *Ibid*, 24
3. *Ibid*, 34
4. *Ibid*, 36
5. *Ibid*, 55
6. *Ibid*, 56–57
7. *Ibid*, 94
8. The British Library catalogue lists '*The Pocket Companion and Penny Guide to the Crystal Palace,* 1854 by Selim Aga (pseud)'. This copy was destroyed during the Blitz and no other has been traced; the identity of the author remains unconfirmed.
9. de Vries, 68 *et seq*
10. Jeal, 22
11. McCarthy, (2004 b)1
12. Aga, (1853) 9
13. Altick, 236–37
14. *Ibid*, 204
15. *Ibid*, 208
16. *Ibid*, 206
17. Aga, (1853) 8
18. Altick, 422
19. McCarthy, (2004 a) 209–10
20. Aga, (1853) 10–11
21. *Ibid*, 11

CHAPTER NINE

Exploring the Niger

1. Mountfield, 67
2. *Ibid*, 72
3. *Ibid*, 81–84
4. de Gramont, 218
5. *Ibid*, 227
6. Burton, (1875) 204
7. Burton, (1863 a) vol 1, 10
8. Lloyd, 190
9. Mathew & Harrison, 252
10. Lloyd, 199
11. Crowther & Taylor, xi–xii
12. Hastings, 18
13. *Ibid*, 57
14. *Ibid*, 60 *et seq*
15. Crowther & Taylor, 75
16. Lloyd, 200
17. Crowther & Taylor, 106
18. Hastings, 107–12
19. *Ibid*, 113
20. *Ibid*, 206

21. Crowther & Taylor, 153
22. Glover, 79–80
23. Lloyd, 204

CHAPTER TEN
'He took all the trouble of life off my hands'

1. Mathew & Harrison, 34–39
2. *Geographical Magazine*, Feb 1 1877, 43–44
3. FO84/1221 & FO8/1176, 1862
4. Burton, (1863 a) vol 1, 9–10
5. Burton, (1875) 204
6. Wilkins, 202–03
7. McCarthy, (2004 a) 168–70
8. Farwell, 210
9. Burton, (1863 a) vol 1, 22

CHAPTER ELEVEN
Selim Hoists the Union Jack

1. Burton, (1863 a) vol 1, 62
2. Kew Gardens Archives, folio 291, 387–90.
3. Burton, (1863 a) vol 1, 76
4. *Ibid*, 96
5. Underhill, 112
6. Burton, (1863 a) vol 1, 164
7. *Ibid*, 122
8. *Ibid*, 136–37
9. *Ibid*, 163
10. FO 8/1176, 1862
11. Burton, (1863 a) vol 1, 200
12. *Ibid*, 218
13. *Ibid*, 222

CHAPTER TWELVE
'Selim behaved like a trump'

1. Burton, (1876) vol 1, 113
2. *Ibid*, 26
3. *Ibid*, 138
4. *Ibid*, 113–32
5. *Ibid*, 174
6. *Ibid*, 176
7. Burton, (1863 b) 139–40
8. *Ibid*, 141
9. *Ibid*, 157
10. *Ibid*, 273
11. *Ibid*, 280–81
12. *Ibid*, 286–87
13. *Ibid*, 287–88
14. *Ibid*, 407
15. *Ibid*, 413
16. *Ibid*, 417
17. *Ibid*, 418–19
18. Burton (1876) 81
19. Aga, (1875) 204
20. Burton 1876, 265
21. *Ibid*, 199
22. *Ibid*, 303
23. Aga, (1875) 207
24. Burton, (1876) 298

CHAPTER THIRTEEN
Two Thousand 'Amazons'

1. Forbes, 207–09
2. FO 84/1203 private letter 31 May 1864
3. FO /284

CHAPTER FOURTEEN
The Last Adventure

1. Glover, ER, 79

Index

Some other books published by **LUATH** PRESS

Wild Scotland: Essential Guide to the Best of Natural Scotland
James McCarthy
ISBN 1 84282 096 6
PBK £8.99

Where are you most likely to see otters in Scotland?
When is the best time to see Scotland's orchids?
In which city can you see fossil trees over 300 million years old?
Where can you be guaranteed to see, at close quarters, a peregrine feeding its chicks?

Wild Scotland, the site by site guide to the best of natural Scotland, answers these and many other questions.

This book is a fascinating overview of the animals, plants, birds and marine creatures which populate the beautiful countryside of Scotland. With indispensable advice on where to go and when, how to see the wildlife, how best to photograph it, and what you can do to help conserve the unspoilt land you visit, this revised and updated edition of James McCarthy's classic guide to the Scottish wilderness is essential reading for tourist and local alike.

Photographs by Laurie Campbell.
Introduction by Magnus Magnusson.

'Beautifully illustrated with line drawings and wonderful photographs... this comprehensive, pocket-sized guide is an excellent companion for walkers, naturalists or lovers of Scotland's natural assets.'
ASSOCIATION FOR THE PROTECTION OF RURAL SCOTLAND

Scotland – Land and People: An Inhabited Solitude
James McCarthy
ISBN 0 946487 57 X
PBK £7.99

The new Scottish Parliament is responsible for the environment of Scotland with the opportunity for land reform and new approaches to the protection and management of an incomparable countryside to meet the needs of the 21st century.

It is difficult to avoid the conclusion that a far more radical approach is now required to safeguard the public interest over a very large proportion of Scotland's mountain and moorland country. There is little point in exhorting the unemployed, trapped in sub-standard inner city homes, to support campaigns for sustainable forestry or the protection of the Green Belt from industrial encroachment.

The plain fact of the matter is that in Scotland, as elsewhere, the means of subsistence will always be first priority where this is under threat, and so-called environmentalists have too often been guilty of adopting an indifference to this.

Bad Ass Raindrop
Kokumo Rocks
ISBN 1 84282 018 4
PBK £6.99

What would happen if a raindrop took acid?
Does your bum shake and does your belly wobble?
And have you noticed that there are no black babies on 'New Baby' cards?

Fadeke Kokumo Rocks' poetry is alive with love, passion, humour and brutal honesty. It is sharply observed, potent and insightful, capturing beautifully the sixth dimension of the creative eye. It has a rich diversity of time and content which embraces the globe and its conflicts, domestic and urban.

You can hear the monsoon rains of Africa, taste the mangoes of India, touch the compassion and spirit of the child and sense the pain of burning flesh as race riots rage.

Read the eclectic, electrifying poetry of Kokumo Rocks in this collection containing over 30 of her most popular poems. Full of Kokumo's distinctive humour, *Bad Ass Raindrop* challenges the questions we answer unquestioning.

'Rocks' work speaks of Africa and India... of racism, injustice and black pride. But she refuses to confine herself to discussions of race. There are waves and beaches, Leith schoolgirls, sex, shopping, AIDS and raindrops that take acid.'
THE HERALD

Think Global, Act Local: the Life and Legacy of Patrick Geddes
ed. Walter Stephen
ISBN 1 84282 079 6
PBK £12.99

Town planning. Interest-led, open-minded education. Preservation of buildings with historical worth. Community gardens. All are so central to modern society that our age tends to claim these notions as its own. In fact they were first visualised by Sir Patrick Geddes, a largely forgotten Victorian Scot and one of the greatest forward thinkers in history.

Gardener, biologist, conservationist, social evolutionist, peace warrior, and town planner, Geddes spent many years conserving and restoring Edinburgh's historic Royal Mile at a time when most decaying buildings were simply torn down. With renovation came educational ideas such as the development of the Outlook Tower, numerous summer schools and his Collège des Écossais in Montpellier. In India much of Geddes's belief in people planning can be seen, taking the form of pedestrian zones, student accommodation for women, and urban diversification projects.

Walter Stephen examines the life of this man who in recent years has become almost a patron saint of the sustainable development movement, and the continuing relevance of his ideas and their place in our world, present and future.

Not Nebuchadnezzar: In Search of Identities
Jenni Calder
ISBN 1 84282 060 5
PBK £9.99

This is a biography, of sorts, and a description of the all-consuming search for that elusive concept known as 'identity'.

Jenni Calder was born Jennifer Rachel Daiches to a Scottish-born mother and English-born Jewish father in Chicago, one of America's great melting-pot cities. This book traces her journey from then to now, a journey that has taken her from America to Scotland via Cambridge, Israel and Kenya, with stops all over the world along the way during her travels as a writer. Throughout her travels, Calder discovers that 'knowing who she is' is only the first step - her true sense of identity develops from finding out who she is not.

This idea of who you are not informing your identification of who you are, and the struggle to find and establish one's identity, will be understood by displaced people and those without the traditional idea of 'roots' from around the world.

'...explores aspects of her life in a series of lucid, thoughtful essays which examine the concept of identity.'
THE SCOTSMAN

Bare Feet and Tackety Boots
Archie Cameron
ISBN 0 946487 17 0
PBK £7.95

The last survivor of those who were born and raised on the island of Rum before the First World War tells his story. Factors and schoolmasters, midges and poaching, deer, ducks and McBrayne's steamers; here social history and personal anecdote create a record of a way of life gone not long ago but already almost forgotten. This is the story the gentry couldn't tell.

'The authentic breath of the country-wise estate employee.'
THE OBSERVER

'An important piece of social history. An insight into how the other half lived in an era the likes of which will never be seen again.'
FORTHRIGHT MAGAZINE

RUSSELL LYON

Vet in the Country

Vet in the Country

Russell Lyon

ISBN 1 84282 067 2
PBK £9.99

From the Borders of Scotland to the Norfolk Fens, Russell Lyon shares his lifetime's experiences as a country vet. From midnight call-outs to cows giving birth on the roof, Vet in the Country is full of memorable anecdotes and observations drawn from Russell's nearly forty years in the field as a vet in rural Britain.

Describing how his early years on a Scottish farm led to his career in veterinary medicine, Russell uses warmth and humour to share his love of animals and convey to the reader the many trials and tribulations he has experienced as a vet. From his first day on the job being taught how to lasso an oil drum, to his thoughts on current veterinary trends and farming practices, Russell Lyon's *Vet in the Country* is an entertaining and absorbing memoir from an established and respected countryside vet.

'It is based upon many years' experience as a practicing vet, experience that means that, though this book is often amusing, it is also sobering.'
EVERGREEN QUARTERLY

Tobermory Teuchter

Peter Macnab

ISBN 0 946487 41 3
PBK £7.99

Peter Macnab was reared on Mull, as was his father, and his grandfather before him. In this book he provides a revealing account of life on Mull during the first quarter of the 20th century, focussing especially on the years of World War I. This enthralling social history of the island is set against Peter Macnab's early years as the son of the governor of Mull Poorhouse, one of the last in the Hebrides, and is illustrated throughout by photographs from his exceptional collection. Peter Mcnab's 'fisherman's yarns' and other personal reminiscences are told delightfully by a born storyteller.

'Peter Macnab is a man of words who doesn't mince his words - not where his beloved Mull is concerned. "I will never forget some of the inmates of the poorhouse," says Peter. "Some of them were actually victims of the later Clearances. It was history at first hand, and there was no romance about it." But Peter Macnab sees little creative point in crying over ancient injustices. For him the task is to help Mull in this century and beyond.'
SCOTS MAGAZINE

Scots in the USA
Jenni Calder
ISBN 1 905222 06 8
PBK £8.99

The map of the United States is peppered with Scottish placenames and America's telephone directories are filled with surnames illustrating Scottish ancestry. Increasingly, Americans of Scottish extraction are visiting Scotland in search of their family history. All over Scotland and the United States there are clues to the Scottish-American relationship, the legacy of centuries of trade and communication as well as that of departure and heritage.

The experiences of Scottish settlers in the United States varied enormously, as did their attitudes to the lifestyles that they left behind and those that they began anew once they arrived in North America.

Scots in the USA discusses why they left Scotland, where they went once they reached the United States, and what they did when they got there.

'. . . a valuable readable and illuminating addition to a burgeoning literature. . . should be required reading on the flight to New York by all those on the Tartan Week trail.'
Alan Taylor, SUNDAY HERALD

Scots in Canada
Jenni Calder
ISBN 1 84282 038 9
PBK £7.99

In Canada there are nearly as many descendants of Scots as there are people living in Scotland; almost five million Canadians ticked the 'Scottish origin' box in the most recent Canadian Census. Many Scottish families have friends or relatives in Canada.

Thousands of Scots were forced from their homeland, while others chose to leave, seeking a better life. As individuals, families and communities, they braved the wild Atlantic ocean, many crossing in cramped under-rationed ships, unprepared for the fierce Canadian winter. And yet Scots went on to lay railroads, found banks and exploit the fur trade, and helped form the political infrastructure of modern day Canada.

'meticulously researched and fluently written… it neatly charts the rise of a country without succumbing to sentimental myths'
SCOTLAND ON SUNDAY

'Calder celebrates the ties that still bind Canada and Scotland in camaraderie after nearly 400 years of relations'
THE CHRONICLE

This City Now: Glasgow and its working class past
Ian R Mitchell
ISBN 1 84282 082 6
PBK £12.99

This City Now sets out to retrieve the hidden architectural, cultural and historical riches of some of Glasgow's working-class districts. Many who enjoy the fruits of Glasgow's recent gentrification will be surprised and delighted by the gems which Ian Mitchell has uncovered beyond the usual haunts.

An enthusiastic walker and historian, Mitchell invites us to recapture the social and political history of the working-class in Glasgow, by taking us on a journey from Partick to Rutherglen, and Clydebank to Pollokshaws, revealing the buildings which go unnoticed every day yet are worthy of so much more attention.

Once read and inspired, you will never be able to walk through Glasgow in the same way again.

'...both visitors and locals can gain instruction and pleasure from this fine volume... Mitchell is a knowledgable, witty and affable guide through the streets of the city.'
GREEN LEFT WEEKLY

The Highland Clearances Trail
Rob Gibson
ISBN 1 905222 10 6
PBK £5.99

It is obvious there is a need for an investigation into the nature and scale of the Highland Clearances. The facts have always been subject to revision, but now Rob Gibson's *The Highland Clearances Trail* systematically documents dates, places, names and numbers and in doing so nails the lie the Clearances were somehow a benevolent act by paternalistic landowners.

Answers the where, why, what and whens of the Highland Clearances and provides an alternative route around the Highlands that will leave the reader with a deeper understanding of this sublime landscape.

'It is important to get the whole movement into perspective and examine the truth of the matter and I hope that this well-written book will address the balance.'
HIGHLAND NEWS

NATURAL WORLD

The Hydro Boys: pioneers of renewable energy
Emma Wood
ISBN 1 84282 047 8 PBK £8.99

Red Sky at Night
John Barrington
ISBN 0 946487 60 X PBK £8.99

Listen to the Trees
Don MacCaskill
ISBN 0 946487 65 0 PBK £9.99

SOCIAL HISTORY

Pumpherston: The story of a shale oil village
Sybil Cavanagh
ISBN 1 84282 011 7 HBK £17.99
ISBN 1 84282 015 X PBK £10.99

Shale Voices
Alistair Findlay
ISBN 0 946487 78 2 HBK £17.99
ISBN 0 946487 63 4 PBK £10.99

Crofting Years
Francis Thompson
ISBN 0 946487 06 5 PBK £6.95

Hail Philpstoun's Queen
Barbara and Marie Pattullo
ISBN 1 84282 094 X HBK £15.99
ISBN 1 84282 095 8 PBK £6.99

Tunnel Tigers
Patrick Campbell
ISBN 1 84282 072 9 PBK £8.99

HISTORY

Scotch on the Rocks: The true story behind Whisky Galore
Arthur Swinson
ISBN 1 905222 09 2 PBK £7.99

Reportage Scotland: Scottish history in the voices of those who were there
Louise Yeoman
ISBN 1 84282 051 6 PBK £7.99

Desire Lines: A Scottish Odyssey
David R Ross
ISBN 1 84282 033 8 PBK £9.99

A Passion for Scotland
David R Ross
ISBN 1 84282 019 2 PBK £5.99

FOLKLORE

Luath Storyteller: Highland Myths & Legends (new edition)
George W Macpherson
ISBN 1 84282 064 8 PBK £5.99

Luath Storyteller: Tales of the Picts
Stuart McHardy
ISBN 1 84282 097 4 PBK £5.99

ART AND ARTISTS

Monsieur Mackintosh: Charles Rennie Mackintosh in/en Roussillon
Robin Crichton
ISBN 1 905222 36 X PBK £15.00

Details of these and all other books we publish can be found online at **www.luath.co.uk**

Luath Press Limited

committed to publishing well written books worth reading

LUATH PRESS takes its name from Robert Burns, whose little collie Luath (*Gael.*, swift or nimble) tripped up Jean Armour at a wedding and gave him the chance to speak to the woman who was to be his wife and the abiding love of his life. Burns called one of *The Twa Dogs* Luath after Cuchullin's hunting dog in Ossian's *Fingal*. Luath Press was established in 1981 in the heart of Burns country, and is now based a few steps up the road from Burns' first lodgings on Edinburgh's Royal Mile. Luath offers you distinctive writing with a hint of unexpected pleasures. Most bookshops in the UK, the US, Canada, Australia, New Zealand and parts of Europe, either carry our books in stock or can order them for you. To order direct from us, please send a £sterling cheque, postal order, international money order or your credit card details (number, address of cardholder and expiry date) to us at the address below. Please add post and packing as follows: UK – £1.00 per delivery address; overseas surface mail – £2.50 per delivery address; overseas airmail – £3.50 for the first book to each delivery address, plus £1.00 for each additional book by airmail to the same address. If your order is a gift, we will happily enclose your card or message at no extra charge.

ILLUSTRATION: IAN MCKELLAS

Luath Press Limited
543/2 Castlehill
The Royal Mile
Edinburgh
EH1 2ND
Scotland
Telephone: 0131 225 4326 (24 hours)
Fax: 0131 225 4324
email: sales@luath.co.uk
Website: www.luath.co.uk